THE
FAMILY
CAMPER'S
BIBLE

Bill Riviere

THE
FAMILY
CAMPER'S
BIBLE

DOUBLEDAY & COMPANY, INC.

GARDEN CITY, NEW YORK   1975

Library of Congress Cataloging in Publication Data

Riviere, William A
   The family camper's bible.

   Includes bibliographical references.
      1. Camping.   2. Recreational vehicles.   I. Title.
GV191.7.R58   796.54
ISBN 0-385-01779-0
Library of Congress Catalog Card Number 71–12734

Contents

Introduction

No one more easily takes to the woods than the family camper. He drives directly to his campsite and sets up his outfit, including the portable luxuries that all too often draw sneers from so-called "rough-it, real campers," and the subsequent trite remarks about "wall-to-wall coffee pots" or "everything but the kitchen sink." As a matter of fact, family campers *do* bring along the kitchen sink! But their mode of camping needs no defense.

What is needed is a re-education of the critics of family camping. This form of outdoor recreation involves no particular challenge. Nature doesn't become an adversary. There is no precipitous cliff to be scaled, no pitch of wild water to be run, no vast distances to be trudged. There are no heavy odds. Family camping is a low-key, restrained enjoyment of the outdoors.

After all, family campers are just that—families—with children who may range from nursing infants to restless teen-agers. The younger the family, the less inclined it is toward a true wilderness experience. And this is wise. The father's total exposure to outdoor life may have consisted solely of two weeks at Scout camp; and a young suburban mother who broils lamb chops electronically at home isn't about to concoct a freeze-dried goulash over a campfire halfway up Moose Mountain in the rain! Her prime concern is the well-being of her family. Camping adventure comes second.

Family campers are a gregarious lot, too. Admittedly, most would like to see a thinning of the crowds on overburdened campgrounds, but they rarely want to be alone. They *like* people. This attitude closely parallels that of the pioneers who crossed the plains in covered wagons, joining forces at common camping grounds and en route, not only for protection, but for companionship, to trade goods and information, and for mutual assistance. This interdependence prevails among family campers. If you're having trouble spotting your rig or setting up your tent, chances are a dozen nearby campers will stroll over to help. And nowhere in the world is more information (especially about campgrounds!) traded than at a family campers' coffee klatch!

Families rarely invade the hinterlands, and seldom penetrate bear country. They know better. But they *do* explore their own environment. They enjoy and learn from established nature trails; they take day trips by canoe or boat, climb moderate mountains over the easier trails, and delight in observing wildlife, whether it's a chipmunk or a deer. They even go walking in a warm summer rain.

And to the glee of the children, you'll find them camped near to, and visiting, such places as Walt Disney World, Old Faithful, Santa Claus Land, or a ghost town. You'll see them at Gettysburg, too, and at the Lincoln Memorial, at Little Big Horn, absorbing the rich heritage of our past. Look for them at county fairs, country auctions, and at local festivals. They are more than tourists. They are living participants in today's America.

However, as I write this, the country has just emerged from the early-1974 "gasoline crisis," which threw the recreational vehicle industry into a major tizzy and had family campers wondering if their next vacation might be spent in the driveway.

It may be that, as you read this, the gasoline problem has been resolved and that high-speed crisscrossing of the continent has resumed. On the other hand, energy experts insist that the shortage will not soon be completely overcome, perhaps never, but certainly not before we attain our energy independence sometime about 1980. Nor, we're told, is the price of gasoline likely to drop back to its precrisis level. The outlook is for the opposite: higher prices.

But certain fringe benefits lie in the shadows of this bleak outlook. For example, more camping and less driving, with greater emphasis on the basic reason for a camping trip: being outdoors! By camping closer to home and remaining longer in a given campsite, as opposed to the campground hopping of the past, higher gasoline costs will seem less ominous, rigs will last longer, and the highway pace will be more leisurely. No longer will getting to a campground be like driving in the Indianapolis 500! Then, too, less electrical energy is consumed in camp than at home. All in all, however long they persist, limited gasoline supplies may prove a boon.

Family camping can still mean the dancing of the northern lights, the dissolving hues of a sunset over the lake, the screeching of children reaching for a giant bullfrog as it plops under a lily pad. It can still mean the come-and-get-it aroma of coffee blending with that of pine smoke drifting across campsites at twilight.

Camping will continue to lend a new vigor to family life, to bring people together in a mutual sharing of learning and contentment. It will still nurture a closeness between persons, between families, creeds, and races. Can we ask any more of any human activity?

B.R.

THE
FAMILY
CAMPER'S
BIBLE

Chapter 1

TENTS

Don't let anyone convince you that tents are "going out of style" or that "only kids and mountain climbers use them." True, they show up only in limited numbers on the electrified parking lots we call "campgrounds," but in the hinterlands, where the evening campfire still draws a larger audience than "I Love Lucy," tents dominate.

The appeal lies in the cloth shelter's role as a basic, fundamental haven in the wilds, symbolizing life in its simplest form, bridging time back to the days when man lived with nature instead of bulldozing her. Among tenters, pride is in their style of camping, not in their rigs.

Tents are practical, too. They're economical, certainly; and flexible—almost any spot can be a campsite, and even the heavier family-type tents can be carried a short distance away from road traffic. A tent, even on a crowded campground, spells adventure, especially to youngsters.

But it can't be denied that canvas has shortcomings. Setting up or breaking camp in a downpour rarely rates as a joyful occasion. And a three-day rain will try the souls of parents with two or three young children. To a true tenter, however, this is all part of the game.

Buying your first tent can be a baffling experience. Prices range from $29 to $290; sizes and shapes vary; fabrics are designated by unintelligible decimals: 7.68, 6.73, or 10.10; colorful but deceptive trade names are touted; all of the Madison Avenue gobbledygook seems aimed at would-be tenters.

Two simple rules, however, can guide you:

1. Buy from a dealer who specializes in outdoor gear. His clientele is limited; he can afford to displease very few customers. He is a specialist, as opposed to a tent salesman in a discount house, who will go back to selling power tools or snow blowers when the camping rush ceases. If you believe that the outlandishly low prices offered by shopping center seasonal opportunists are genuine tent bargains, you are naïve.

2. Unless the fabric is clearly labeled, or the clerk can identify it to your satisfaction, hurry to the nearest exit. Labeling laws are of little help, since they call only for general specifications, such as "100 per cent cotton." Frankly, so are my T-shirts, whose fabric hardly qualifies as tentage!

FABRICS

You need concern yourself with only four fabrics: duck, drill or twill, poplin (all of these cotton), and nylon.

First, however, you should know about "breathability" and "finish." Even when you're inactive—asleep, in fact—your body daily gives off more than a pint of moisture, often termed "insensitive perspiration." This moisture must pass off through the tent fabric during the night into the atmosphere. If your tent is truly waterproof, this moisture cannot escape, and it condenses upon striking the cool tent roof and walls. During the summer, small puddles will form in the tent. In cold weather, you'll find ice inside your shelter! A tent fabric, therefore, must not be waterproof. It should be *water-repellent*.

Cotton—duck, drill (or twill), and poplin—are water-repellent because when wet by rain, the fibers in the weave swell and tighten. In addition, a "finish" is applied to tent cottons that will help repel rain, yet allow the passage of interior moisture to the outside. This is a neat trick, but the textile industry has managed it.

Two types of "finish" are applied to tent fabrics: "wet" and "dry." The wet finish is common in less expensive tents and consists mainly of paraffin, easily identified by its smell. Such fabrics stiffen in cold weather, and go limp under a hot sun. Color rubs off, and dirt clings to the tacky surface. My own tests have proven to my satisfaction that such fabrics are highly susceptible to mildew, despite "mildew resistant" labels. A clue to such finishes lies in catalogs that specify the weight of fabrics as "7.68 ounces before treatment." The paraffin's weight can add up to 50 per cent, so that a 7.68-ounce material probably weighs more than 10 ounces.

A dry finish, on the other hand, adds little or no weight. The fabric remains soft and pliable, has no odor, repels grit, and its color will fade only very slowly, without rubbing off. Dry finishes are trade secrets and are costlier than paraffin treatments. They are applied to all cotton tentage but only in the better-quality models.

Whichever you buy is a matter your budget must decide. If your financial situation is snug, don't forgo camping because you can't afford a dry-finish tent. A paraffin-treated tent simply requires greater care to prevent mildew. This means dismantling every three or four days, or at least lifting the floor and wall hems off the ground long enough to dry. This is the area where mildew and rot problems originate.

If you decide in favor of a dry-finish tent, don't be alarmed if a fine mist seeps through during your first or second exposure to rain. The weave will "settle in," eliminating this misting. Better yet, set up the tent in your backyard and hose it down gently two or three times, allowing it to dry between wettings.

Probably the most serviceable of all tent fabrics is army duck, woven with both the warp (yarns running lengthwise) and the fill (crosswise yarns) doubled and twisted—these known as "plied" yarns. Army duck is free of sizing, a starch added to inferior materials to lend them body. Hold a piece of army duck up to a strong light and you will see that the yarns are uniformly spun, evenly and tightly woven—so tightly, in fact, that the fabric is water-repellent even when untreated—yet it will breathe. Most army duck tents made for family campers are made of 10.10 ounces-per-square-yard fabric. This designation leads some to believe that a 10′×14′ army duck tent must weigh as much as a cast-iron cookstove. The fact is that, since dry-finish yardage is designated by its actual weight, 10-ounce army duck may actually be lighter than so-called "7.68 ounces before treatment" drill.

Army duck is too expensive for an occasional-use tent. It's designed for hard service, week after week, year after year. I have two army duck tents, abused for more than ten years, but still as serviceable as on the day I bought them. Given equal time on the road and in campgrounds, an army duck tent will outlast many a travel trailer!

Drill is the most commonly used tent fabric, and its cost is relatively low. The better grades have a dry finish applied to them; inferior grades are often dubbed with paraffin. In the showroom they are difficult to tell apart unless you're a textile expert. I repeat: Buy from a dealer whose business is tents and who handles well-known brands. Do this, give your tent reasonable care, and you'll get years of service. Buy a "cheapie" and you'll find the floor/wall hem rotting during the first season. Worse yet, the tent will shrink and no longer fit its frame.

Poplin is a dry-finish, high-count (up to 160 threads per square inch) fabric, usually 6 to 8 ounces per square yard. Regrettably, it is often disguised by confusing trade names, although it need not travel incognito. It is a superb, medium-priced combination of lightness and durability.

One note of caution will apply to all cotton fabrics, however—and this includes duck, drill, and poplin. Never store the tent for more than a few days while it is wet. Obviously, there will come a morning when you must break camp in the rain. Don't worry about this, but when you arrive at home, erect the tent in the backyard and allow it to dry thoroughly before storing.

Given enough use, any tent may develop leaks, either localized or in the form of a "misting" over a large area. This can be remedied. In the case of a "wet" finish tent, a "waterproofing" can be applied, this obtainable from most tent dealers. Be sure to specify a "wet" finish. Set up the tent in your yard and apply the waterproofing with a large paintbrush, preferably on a sunny day. Allow the tent to stand two or three days before storage.

In the case of a "dry" finish, the "waterproofing" comes in an aerosol spray can. Set up the tent, spray it thoroughly, roll or fold it loosely, and store it for three to five days in a plastic bag in a warm room. The plastic will confine the spray chemical and allow it to penetrate thoroughly to all parts, including the seams. Remove the plastic and store the tent loosely rolled.

Nylon is another matter. It's incredibly durable, light, and truly mildewproof. Early nylon tents, however, did not "breathe." World War II Alpine troops, among the first users, discovered that their tent interiors "iced up." Attempts at producing family-camping tents after the war ran into the same trouble.

Then came a superlight nylon, weighing less than two ounces per yard, a fabric that did, indeed, breathe! Hundreds of mountaineering tent designs blossomed, some housing two men while weighing less than five pounds! What's more, the fabric withstood winds that would peel the hide off a bull moose. But it would not repel a heavy rain. So tent manufacturers came up with a tent fly of nylon coated with urethane or vinyl, adding only about one pound to the weight of a two-man tent. The fly, being truly waterproof, repelled the heaviest rain, keeping the downpour from striking the tent itself, whose uncoated nylon did breathe. For the backpacker and mountaineer, this proved to be the perfect fabric combination.

Seeking to eliminate the need for a fly, some manufacturers produce mountain tents made entirely of coated nylon, claiming that their models provide ample ventilation to allow dispersal of interior moisture without condensation. Although such tents persist on the market, they are notable failures. Condensation still occurs, for the simple reasons that ventilation is not adequate and that vapors simply cannot be directed into certain openings.

Family campers also benefit from coated nylon, which is used extensively for floors in tents otherwise made of cotton. Such floors are waterproof, of course, will never rot, and can be quickly cleaned with a damp sponge or cloth, a decided advantage over cotton floors, which soiled easily and permanently. A few manufacturers, notably Coleman and Sears, adopted the European "tub bottom," running the nylon floor a few inches up the sidewalls, virtually eliminating mildew at the floor/wall hem.

In 1973 two firms introduced all-nylon tents for family campers in cottage and umbrella models, weighing far less than the conventional cotton shelters, and attractively priced because they are made in Puerto Rico and Japan. I contacted both firms, specifically asking for documentation or test reports that they had overcome the nylon bugaboo of misting without coating, condensation with it.

One firm sent a colorful catalog but ignored my queries. Its catalog portrayed nylon, family-sized tents, made no mention of the condensation problem, nor that of misting, except in its description of "optional" coated nylon flies. It led the would-be buyer to think that the fly is only a worthwhile luxury, not the necessity that it really is.

The other firm answered my queries directly and honestly. Yes, their coated nylon could cause condensation; yes, their nylon tents should be used with a coated fly. My only doubt is that the nylon walls of their tents are coated lightly with urethane. Experience has shown that either a urethane or a vinyl coating has a waterproofing effect.

So, until tent firms are willing to *guarantee* that their new nylon models will perform perfectly with regard to condensation and/or misting, I can only continue to urge the use of duck, drill, and poplin as the best fabrics, with coated nylon as a floor material.

THE UMBRELLA TENT

An exterior-frame umbrella tent can be erected in ten minutes or less, many models requiring neither stakes nor guy lines. A 9'×9' floor size is ample for two persons, almost luxurious in fact, with space for gear. For three to four persons, go to a 12'×12' model, or a model with a side-room extension providing a 10'×14' floor area. For more than four persons, double-extension types have floor areas up to 10'×20'. Only rarely will a tent comfortably accommo-

The Eureka Holiday Space tent, an umbrella style, with top fly. EUREKA TENT AND AWNING COMPANY

date the number of campers claimed. Tent capacities are overrated! Double-deck folding bunks increase sleeping capacity, of course, but aisle traffic may be a little heavy. Buy a tent large enough for your family. Otherwise, you'll have to go outside to roll over!

Consider eave height and width, too, for these are what provide headroom. A 9'×9' tent with 4-foot eaves, for example, will permit less headroom than a tent with 5-foot eaves. As for the height of the eaves, don't settle for less than 5½ feet. Six feet is better.

Setting up an umbrella tent is simplicity itself. The floor is squared, and if required, four corner stakes are driven. Then the top spreader is placed into position over the folded tent. Inserting sectional corner poles into this lifts the tent quickly into position.

The interior centerpole for use in umbrella tents is now virtually obsolete. A few models still utilize interior corner poles, usually of sectional aluminum, often spring-loaded to maintain tension. But these tend to lean with a strong wind, somewhat distorting the tent's shape. Interior suspension systems are difficult to set up since you'll have to work inside the partially erect tent. Under a hot sun, this is not pleasant.

THE WALL TENT

Traditionally a shelter for backcountry campers, usually for a semipermanent camp, the wall tent has found little favor among camping families. It is not easy to erect, and generally does not feature a sewed-in floor (which is standard on the umbrella model, for example). And there are no windows. Most models require an interior ridge pole and numerous guy lines. Older models, and those favored for use in remote areas, have a tape ridge to which are attached tie tapes for suspension on an exterior ridge pole, or shear rig, generally cut at the tent site. These are heavy-duty tents, usually of army duck. A lightweight version of this tent—a 10'×12' model with a 7' ridge height and 3' wall height, weighs about 27 pounds. A sewed-in floor and insect netting are optional, along with a zippered back window. It's produced by the Duluth Tent and Awning Company of Duluth, Minnesota. When you consider that my 9'×13' army

The author's Eureka Holiday umbrella tent on a British Columbia campground. RIVIERE

Interior frame umbrella tent with
rear extension, the Wildwood Forest
View by Laacke and Joys Company.

A modern wall tent with high sidewalls, interior ridge pole, and exterior side frame.
EUREKA TENT AND AWNING COMPANY

Still higher sidewalls provide for ample headroom in this cottage-type tent patterned after a wall tent. EUREKA TENT AND AWNING COMPANY

The Continental, a cottage-type tent. SEARS, ROEBUCK AND COMPANY

duck wall tent, similarly equipped, weighs more than 60 pounds, the Duluth version is a tentmaker's triumph.

All in all, family campers will find the wall tent a superb shelter for a semipermanent encampment, a 9'×12' model accommodating four persons with cots placed along the low walls, leaving the center aisle for "traffic." But for "one-night stands" or for a tent that must be moved frequently, a better choice would be an umbrella or cottage model.

THE COTTAGE TENT

Someone once pointed out that a cottage or cabin tent is nothing more than a wall tent with high sidewalls and, I suppose, that's about as accurate a description as any. The roof pitch isn't as steep, but the high walls make possible windows almost completely around the shelter. Most cottage tents use a combination of interior and exterior suspension. After staking out the four corners, outside poles prop up the sides to eave height. Two interior uprights and the ridge pole are then set in place, not a difficult chore but one usually requiring two persons. One of the newer versions of the cottage tent has an exterior ridge pole suspended on a completely exterior frame, simplifying the chore of setting up.

Cottage tents range in size from 9'×11' up to

The cottage tent is suspended on a completely exterior frame, making it easy to erect. WENZEL TENT AND DUCK COMPANY

10'×18'. There isn't much point to buying the smaller versions since umbrella tents have almost the same capacity and are easier to erect. For larger families, however, one of the bigger "cottages" can be set up literally as a "bunkhouse," easily sleeping twelve or more persons by using double-deck folding aluminum cots. Wall height in these tents runs from 4' up to 6'. Another advantage of the cottage tent is that screened enclosures are easily added, often doubling the capacity of the shelter, either for additional sleeping space or as a kitchen or lounging area.

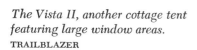

The Vista II, another cottage tent featuring large window areas. TRAILBLAZER

A pioneer among Quonset-type tents, the Prairie Schooner. It uses Fiberglas rods for suspension. THERMOS

THE QUONSET TENT

Reminiscent of World War II Quonset huts, these tents offer essentially the same floor area as wall tents. However, they provide greater headroom, have fewer stakes and guy lines, are much easier to erect, and are stable in a wind. Suspension is by means of flexible Fiberglas sectional struts inserted into exterior sleeves.

One version of this tent, the Thermos Prairie Schooner, is made of 8-ounce dry-finish drill, a superb medium-priced fabric. Another version is the Winchester Trailblazer Atlantis, made of 7.68-ounce poplin with a sewed-in coated nylon floor. These are colorful and striking camping shelters. And they're highly practical.

THE BAKER TENT

The Baker is a lean-to, with a rear wall and a drop-canopy fully opening front. Modern versions have sewed-in floors and full front screening, plus a rear window. Generally it is smaller than most family camping tents, running about 7'×8'. Headroom is at a minimum, usually 6' at the

The Atlantis, a dramatic version of the Quonset-type tent suspended on aluminum rods within fabric sleeves. TRAILBLAZER/WINCHESTER

Old-style Baker tent, still popular in backwoods camping and as an auxiliary tent. NATIONAL CANVAS PRODUCTS

front and 2′ at the rear. One of my happy recollections about the Baker is going to sleep while watching the firelight playing on the sloping top, reflected through the open front. We lost something when we started zippering ourselves in for the night. The Baker serves primarily as a sleeping shelter, but some families use it for a second tent in which they set up a table for dining—which makes for posh camping, especially in bad weather. Usually it is suspended by four corner poles, with some models utilizing a ridge pole also.

THE POP TENT

An igloo-shaped shelter, 9′ in diameter and 6′6″ high, the Pop tent is popular among small families, and it serves well as an auxiliary tent. Sectional Fiberglas rods, like those used in the Quonset tent, fit into exterior sleeves and literally "pop" the tent open. No guy lines or stakes are required, although provisions for guying are included. I've found the tent remarkably stable and durable, the fabric a good-quality, dry-finish drill.

Two versions of the famed Pop tent, a 7- and a 9-footer. THERMOS

The five sizes of Draw-Tite tents, the 8′×10′ and the 9′×12′ at the right, best suited for family camping. EUREKA TENT AND AWNING COMPANY

THE DRAW-TITE TENT

This tent is unique, made only by the Eureka Tent and Awning Company of Binghamton, New York. Of 6½-ounce poplin, it is suspended entirely by means of an exterior frame consisting of interchangeable aluminum rods. Elastic shock cord keeps the fabric taut but never applies undue stress. No stakes or guy lines are required. In fact, the entire tent can be picked up as a unit and moved after being erected. The floor is coated nylon. The 8′×10′ model weighs only 30 pounds; the 9′×12′ model, slightly over 33 pounds. The manufacturer claims it can be set up in four minutes, probably accurate timing once you're thoroughly familiar with it. My best was slightly over six minutes, hardly a horrendous chore! The invention of Robert L. Blanchard, five sizes are available, the larger two noted above, best suited for family camping.

AUXILIARY TENTS

A second tent may well solve the problem of an overcrowded family tent. Several are suitable for such use, the pup tent probably the most popular. I nurture an intense hatred for this canvas doghouse as a shelter for adults, but it is entirely adequate for sleeping two youngsters.

The GI version, without floor or insect netting, is unsuitable, but many commercial models offer these refinements at low cost. The pup tent is, in fact, the least expensive of all camping shelters. Some, however, are little more than play tents, which will not withstand the rigors of camping. Choose one of the better ones, preferably of 7.68-ounce drill. Anything less sturdy than this is a poor investment.

Other excellent "second tents" are the 7-foot pop tent, suspended much like its larger counterpart already described, and inexpensive varieties of the explorer, the A or wedge, the miner's, and the so-called hiker's tents. While these should be equipped with sewed-in floor and insect netting, you need not invest in the high-grade versions of these shelters, which are designed for serious camping during backcountry trips. Several firms make popularly priced models for family campers.

FABRIC COLORS

Color in a tent fabric is not entirely a matter of taste. White canvas, for example, acts as a screen for nighttime silhouettes when a lantern is used inside. Reds and blues, so attractive on the showroom floor, fade rapidly. Yellow and orange, although they do not fade as readily, are considered a mite garish for camping. Dark greens and gray are popular—and with good reason—since they resist fading, do not "shadow," and, even when soiled, remain neat-looking. Olive drab and khaki, once standard colors along with white, have practically disappeared from the camping scene, although an offshoot, suntan, is still much in evidence.

A modern pup tent with sewed-in floor and netting, ideal for children, and as auxiliary.

IMPORTANT INCIDENTALS

Windows and doors should be zippered. Snaps or cloth ties permit gaps and access by insects. If the slide fastener is metal, a No. 7 is more than adequate. It took me some time to accept the somewhat smaller nylon zippers because they seem flimsy, but a recent experience with a new Laacke & Joys Explorer tent convinced me of the durability of nylon. Whether metal or nylon, the zipper should have double tabs so that it can be closed from inside as well as out.

I've never known a snake to enter a tent, but it probably has happened. If this possibility bothers you, seek a tent with a cloth threshold, these usually 3″ to 6″ high, and which can be zippered shut along the bottom of the door. If the threshold can also be dropped, this facilitates sweeping out.

Better tents, particularly umbrella models, are equipped with a storm flap, which may be rolled up and tied over the door under the canopy. Less desirable is the tent that uses the canopy for a storm flap, since during a storm this eliminates the covered "entryway" when it is most needed. Some canopies, too, are rather skimpy, being only slightly wider than the door itself, affording only negligible protection against wind-driven rain. A more suitable canopy is as wide as the tent's front wall.

Adequate ventilation calls for at least one window on each side, and these as large as possible. Cheap shelters are likely to shortchange you on window area. These should be screened, of course, and equipped with storm flaps, which can be closed from inside the tent. One trip in your pajamas into a night storm to close windows from the outside will convince you of this.

Experts used to insist upon a lap-felled seam, in which the two edges of the fabric were folded, then interlocked before being double-sewed. Labor costs have virtually eliminated this seam in

The author has used this tent several times as a canoe trip shelter, but it also serves well as a second tent for families. EUREKA

tentage. However, modern threads now make the flat, overlap seam more than adequate when double-sewed.

All stress points, such as corner, peaks, and ridges, should be reinforced with double layers of fabric. Where grommets are inserted, double layers are necessary.

Beckets are often troublesome. These are the loops at the foot of the tent wall, through which stakes are driven. The best beckets consist of quarter-inch manila rope run through two grommets to form the loop. Replacing these is a matter of minutes, especially convenient since beckets are the first part of a tent to deteriorate, often during the first season. Unfortunately, rope beckets have been replaced by fabric scraps, doubled and looped, then sewed to the hem, where they quickly start to rot since stakes hold them close to the earth's moisture. Nylon fabric is a welcome improvement, since it will not rot and, if properly sewed to the tent, will provide long service.

Another symbol of twentieth-century technology is the plastic stake. When a batch of these arrived recently, I tried them out in various soils surrounding my home and was surprised to find them at least as durable as aluminum pegs. However, I discarded them—because they were only 6″ long! In a hard-packed surface they might be suitable, but they can never anchor a tent safely in soft, forest humus. I've reverted to my 12″ steel stakes.

Unless you're willing to lay out a couple of weeks' salary, there is no perfect tent. The features I've suggested are guidelines; you prob-ably won't find them in any one tent. But seek as many of them as your budget will permit. In the long run, you'll be money ahead.

When your new tent arrives, check to see that all poles, lines, and stakes are included. Shortages are rare, but they do occur. Before your first camping trip, set the tent up in your backyard, allowing it to stand two or three days, preferably through at least one rainstorm. If no rain is in sight, wet it down with a garden hose, using a fine spray. This will "set the weave" and help form the shelter to its suspension system. Don't be alarmed if the directions in the carton are baffling. They are supposed to be! And don't be disappointed if it takes you a half hour to set up when the manufacturer claims this to be a six-minute lark. As you become familiar with your tent, your set-up time will decrease.

Once it is set up, examine the tent for defects. It's to the credit of tentmakers that I have never found serious defects in the more than twenty tents I've acquired during the past thirty-five years. But don't take perfection for granted. Check the seams to see that the sewing machine didn't run off the material. Be sure the beckets are sturdily attached. Try the slide fasteners. If they stick, lubricate them by rubbing with a candle. They'll smooth out with use.

If the tent is of cotton—duck, drill, or poplin—and it is not equipped with a shock-cord suspension system, always slack off any guy lines when you anticipate rain. Do so at night, before retiring, too. Humidity will create temporary shrinkage, which might cause a weak seam to part.

Chapter 2

THE WHEELED RIGS

The news media generally refer to any type of a wheeled camping rig as a "camper"—accurate but too general a term. "Recreational vehicle" is also used widely, but it may also include trail bikes, snowmobiles, and all-terrain vehicles, even four-wheel-drive cars and trucks. It's all very confusing.

The accepted authority is the Recreational Vehicle Institute,[1] which serves manufacturers and users. The Institute describes the various units roughly as follows:

Camping trailer. A folding design to be towed by a passenger car or light truck, presenting a low profile while being towed, yet affording the living space of a small cabin when erected. The term "tent trailer" is no longer always applicable, since many have tops and sides of solid materials rather than canvas.

Travel trailers. Popularly known as "hardtops," there are several types. The most common is actually a miniaturized cottage on two wheels, built to be towed by a passenger car or small truck.

Another style has a telescoping mechanism. When closed for travel, it resembles a folded camping trailer. At the campsite, however, the telescopic top and sides rise to provide full headroom and the appearance of a "hardtop."

The aircraft type of travel trailer is easy to spot. Its outer shell is aluminum, usually unpainted, and well streamlined.

A newcomer is the "fifth wheeler." Manufacturers tend to identify this type of unit as completely separate from travel trailer design. It is nevertheless a trailer. Its hitch, patterned after that used by the big highway transports, is mounted in the bed of a pick-up truck.

Truck campers. Also known as a "pick-up camper," since its two variations were designed for use on light trucks. The first is the "slide-in" model, which is carried in the bed or body of a pick-up and which can be removed by means of jacks affixed to the sides. The other style is a "chassis mount." This one is permanently attached to the truck's chassis in place of the bed.

Truck covers. These are simple hoods, or shells designed to afford low-headroom shelter in the truck body.

Motor homes. Not unlike a bus in appearance, these are self-powered units, with living space and the driver's compartment all under one roof. The term "mobile home" is frequently, and wrongly, applied to these. A mobile home is a large trailer unit, usually 10' wide and up to 60' long, used as a semipermanent residence and can be hauled over highways only by special trucks. The motor home is a recreational unit.

A smaller version of the motor home is a unit converted from a delivery-type van, usually with a permanent "bubble top" or a retractable top that can be raised for full headroom.

A similar unit in size is the "chopped van," which retains only the driver's section, or the front end of the van, with the camper mounted on the chassis at the rear. It somewhat resembles a truck camper.

You can pay as little as $400 for a basic camping trailer, or up to $30,000 or more for a posh

[1] See the Appendix.

Camping trailer, also known as a fold-down trailer. STARCRAFT

Travel trailer, or "hardtop." SHASTA

Telescoping trailer. Top lowers for low profile during travel, raises easily at campsite to provide full headroom of regular travel trailer. HI-LO

"Aircraft" or streamlined type of travel trailer. ARGOSY

A 27-foot "fifth wheel" trailer. HYLAND

motor home. Depending upon your tax bracket, either can be a momentous decision.

First, consider how much use your unit will get. If this amounts to an annual two-week vacation, plus a half dozen weekends per year, the expensive motor home is a poor investment. Depreciation alone will approach the cost of staying at a conventional resort for these periods. Add insurance and operating expenses, repairs and upkeep, and you'll find that it may be less expensive to fly to a posh resort for your vacation! However, if you're the let's-go-every-chance-we-get family, a recreational vehicle within your means will prove a sound investment.

At this time little is known about trade-in values. Camping trailers bring little if they've had three to four years' service; this we do know, since this type of unit has been on the market in quantity for more than fifteen years. The truck camper, in good condition, need not be traded. You simply trade the truck. Travel trailers are rarely traded because they're worn out. Owners usually want to upgrade, or buy a larger model. Such units, in good condition, trade well. But motor homes, and vans, are both too new in the automotive field for definite guidelines to have been developed. At this stage the best advice is

to buy wisely—within your means; maintain your unit carefully; get as much use and mileage out of it as possible. An expensive camper sitting idly in the driveway is a poor investment.

As for sitting in the driveway, check local zoning ordinances before buying. Many communities prohibit the parking of recreational vehicles in residential areas. You may have to arrange storage facilities away from your home, or alter your garage to house your camper out of sight.

Bear in mind, too, that a wheeled camper is, by nature, a gregarious rig. Colorful advertising in magazines invariably portrays a unit on the shore of a hidden lake, a snow-capped mountain in the distance, a deer feeding close by, a lush, green meadow in the foreground—and not another soul within miles! This luxury is afforded only to the backpacker and the canoeman! It stands to reason that where you can drive your rig, another can follow, and several others may have preceded you. The bigger and the heavier your unit is, the more you will be confined to well-developed roads and congested campgrounds. Isolation cannot be yours, not on wheels!

Another quaint custom of advertising agencies is the overuse of the word "spaciousness."

They'd lead you to believe that a 22-foot motor home has lounging space the size of the Waldorf-Astoria Grand Ballroom! "Luxury for six to eight persons." "Sleeps six to eight comfortably." "Banquet-sized dinette." These are typical ad misrepresentations. All of these claims may be true, but only if the participants in this luxury living take turns moving about. Our experience with a 21-footer, and a 22-footer, is that most travel trailers and motor homes are truly luxurious for only two persons.

Bear in mind that all but the biggest units are smaller than the average middle-class living room—but in that space you must eat, sleep, lounge, and occasionally go to the bathroom! What's more, meals are prepared, dishes are washed. Visualize, if you will, trying to perform these tasks within one room of your home.

It takes getting used to! All forms of camping are, of course, a compromise in accommodations. If you have a habitual late-riser, don't let him sleep on the dinette-converted-to-a-luxuriously-large bed! His snoring will delay breakfast. And the couple sleeping in the 42-inch "double" bed over the driver's compartment will need a ladder in order to "rise" in the morning. Shrug off the overdone "spaciousness" claims. Four to six persons in a 24-footer must be mighty friendly to get along, especially during an extended trip.

Generally speaking, recreational vehicles are for campers who can tolerate close quarters, who enjoy neighbors.

In shopping for a wheeled camper your choice will, no doubt, be governed primarily by your financial means. Once you've established your price limitations you can then judge the degree of comfort and convenience you want and can afford.

The larger the unit, the more costly it will be to operate. A small camping trailer that will track behind the family car like a shadow will probably reduce your gas mileage by less than a mile per gallon. On the other hand, a large motor home may get only six miles per gallon! Wind

A "slide-in" version of a truck camper. COACHMAN

*A chassis-mount truck camper
can provide increased floor space.*
FRANKLIN

resistance is another gas-eating factor. A boxlike
unit has more wind-resistance than a streamlined or aerodynamic vehicle. We were quite
surprised upon entering our first eastern toll
highway with a motor home that dual wheels
or tandem axles call for higher tolls on many
such roads. Travel trailers, too, often pay extra
tolls.

Once you decide upon the type of vehicle,
interior arrangements should be appraised objectively. A tiny bathroom the size of a phone
booth may seem "cute" and compact "with all
the conveniences" on the showroom floor, only
to become a torture chamber on the road and
in a campground! The other extreme is the unit

with a spacious, superb bathroom, including a
full tub and shower, space that in many instances might be more wisely put to other uses—
closets, for example.

Much the same thinking should go into appraising the kitchen area. If all meals for a
family of four to six persons will be prepared
aboard, maximum cupboard and sideboard space
should be provided, as well as a refrigerator
large enough to hold a reasonable amount of
perishables. The range, too, should be chosen
for maximum utility.

If the dinette is described as "ample for six
persons," try it out. If the family members find
themselves wedged in with elbows pinned to

Truck cap or hood. DODGE

Full-size motor home. SUPERIOR

their sides, how are they going to eat, and how soon will it be before tempers flare?

Storage space is important, of course. A vacation wardrobe for two adults will often fill the closets in most but the largest motor homes or travel trailers. But how about the fishing tackle, golf clubs, children's toys, camera equipment, and the sundry cultch that all of us tote on a holiday trip?

So-called "living space" is invariably little more than the center aisle running the length of the unit, with closets, dinette, bath, and kitchen on one side or the other. For a couple this is usually more than ample, but with chil-

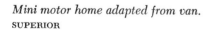

Mini motor home adapted from van. SUPERIOR

"Chopped van" motor home. FAN

dren, this living space must spill over, usually into the dinette or bedroom.

What may be luxuries in smaller vehicles are often necessities in large ones. Dual batteries, for example; the primary to start and operate the engine, the secondary for powering lights and some appliances. A battery isolator is virtually a necessity in this case. It permits the generator or alternator to charge both batteries, but isolates the primary when the engine is shut off, thus assuring that the engine will start in the morning. A power inverter permits the use of both 12 and 110–15 volts. Air conditioning is often regarded as a luxury, but during the summer the vehicle can become uncomfortably hot without it. In cold weather, motor campers cool off quickly and warm up almost as rapidly, so thermostatic heat controls help level off this variation.

The range of comfort and efficiency available in wheeled campers today may vary from the spartan living afforded by a basic camping trailer to every luxury known to man except a swimming pool and turkish bath, in a posh motor home.

So before deciding on your dream model, perhaps too hastily, pore over the brochures, read and compare specifications, ask advice of friends who own a recreational vehicle, and shop among several dealers. Few campers realize that rigid standards have been imposed upon RV builders, by themselves, as members of the Recreational Vehicle Institute. That these standards are not merely window dressing was proved recently when three manufacturers were dropped from membership for violations of standards. Evidence of membership in RVI and compliance with some five hundred separate requirements is in the form of a small oval seal including the words: "Manufacturer Certifies Compliance with ANSI Standard A119.2 National Electrical Code C1." The rim of the oval bears the words: "Electrical, Plumbing, Heating. Member RVI." Don't interpret this as a guarantee that the vehicle is absolutely perfect in every way. Flaws have not yet been eliminated by technology! But the little plaque does indicate that the manufacturer is complying with established safety standards, to the extent that he agrees to frequent unannounced visits to his plant by RVI inspectors.

INSURANCE[2]

Recreational vehicles are sophisticated and specialized units, and they have sophisticated and specialized insurance needs.

[2] See Chapter 20.

A conveniently arranged kitchen or galley area is especially important. LIFETIME

For motor homes and truck campers, the policy should include:

bodily injury and property damage liability;
medical payments;
deductible comprehensive;
deductible collision;
emergency expense allowance;
uninsured motorist coverage (in most states).

For travel trailer or camping trailer, the policy should include:

comprehensive (or named perils);
disappearing collision deductible;
personal effects coverage (inside and outside the unit);
supplemental vacation liability;
accidental death and dismemberment protection;
emergency expense allowance (with no per-day restrictions);
towing and labor costs;
fire department service charge coverage;
guaranteed renewable.

Any RV owner needs liability protection that pays court costs, premiums on court bonds, attorney's fees, and interest on judgments being appealed. It reimburses you for reasonable expenses (but not loss of earnings) that you incur at the insurance company's request in the defense of a claim and pays for necessary first-aid costs incurred at the time of an accident.

Equally important is physical damage coverage to protect the investment you have in your recreational vehicle.

Whether or not your vehicle is in use year-'round, you should maintain twelve-month protection. If parked or in storage, you could have a loss by fire, explosion, theft, or other accident.

Don't shop price! Actuarial tables are inflexible. If you pay less, you'll get less protection. Insist on an explanation of what types of losses are covered and what losses are not included. Take nothing for granted.

RENTALS

Before buying, you may want to rent a unit similar to the one whose purchase you're contemplating—a wise move.

Rental rates vary with geographical location, season, size of the vehicle, and the degree of luxury equipment included. At this writing, no rental agency in the recreational vehicle field operates in a manner similar to that of Hertz or Avis, under which you may rent a unit in one city and leave in another. Most recreational vehicle rentals require that the unit be returned to the renter.

Most rental agencies require a refundable deposit. In some cases, dealers who rent units will apply all or part of the rental fee toward the purchase price.

Chapter 3

CAMPING TRAILERS

Camping trailers can be towed by any full-sized American car with ease. The lighter models can be handled nicely by all American compacts and virtually all small imports. Unless you decide on a superdeluxe version loaded with extras, a Class I hitch will probably suffice.[1] And you'll need a wiring harness that will hook up the trailer's tail, directional, and clearance lights to the car's system, a chore most garages can perform in twenty minutes.

The camping trailer's economy outshines that of any other recreational vehicle. A basic utility model, to which you can add conventional tenting gear such as a campstove, sleeping bags, and a lantern, may cost under $400. Or you can go the luxury route with an outlay of up to $3,000.

Surveys repeatedly indicate that large numbers of campers want "simple, inexpensive" units. Yet dealers and manufacturers report that buyers "insist" on luxury at added cost. This is gobbledygook, of course, the type you run into in automobile showrooms where the "comfort and convenience extras" can approximate one third the cost of the car you had in mind when you entered. The truth is that spartan model trailers are tucked away in the back of the sales lot. Advertising stresses luxury, appeals to status and ego. If your means are limited, there is a trailer for you. Hang in there, brush off the "extras," and insist on seeing a rig within your price limits. However, if you're inclined toward the posh life, your requirements will be quickly fulfilled!

In either case, a prepurchase study is a sound investment. Send for literature—you'll find ads in camping and trailering magazines. Read the brochures, study the specifications. Do this *before* you visit showrooms. Armed with basic knowledge, think of a camping trailer as a simple box on wheels. Then add the features you want.

At this point you may still wonder if a camping trailer is really the best choice. Its advantages are impressive. Original cost can be low; licensing and local taxes, relatively slight. Towing cuts gas mileage only slightly. The low profile eliminates wind resistance. Your rear view is unimpaired while driving. Setting up is quicker and easier than struggling with a large tent. Wives and mothers who envision "crawly things" as part of tent camping find off-the-ground accommodations appealing. Lighter models can be wheeled by hand into a tight campsite. The folding top occupies only about 25 per cent of the box space, so there is room for other vacation gear. Many models provide access to storage compartments without lifting the top, so that noonday picnic stops are a cinch. The camping trailer, like the more luxurious hard-tops, can be left fully loaded between trips, ready to go in a matter of minutes.

Three materials go into the basic trailer box: aluminum, steel, and Fiberglas, sometimes in combination. Aluminum is light, rustproof, and makes small demands on the car's gas mileage,

[1] A class I hitch is for trailers weighing less than 2,000 pounds and having a tongue weight under 80 pounds; Class II: trailers up to 2,000 pounds, tongue weight under 200. "Tongue weight," also called "hitch weight," is the downward thrust of the trailer tongue on the car's rear end, expressed in pounds.

One of the most popular of all canvas-topped trailers. COX

but it is easily bruised. Steel, while heavier, withstands more abuse, such as accidentally backing into a tree, but is subject to rust. Fiberglas also is inexpensive and rugged, but laminations have been known to "bubble" or blister. Which is best? Frankly, it's the Chevrolet/ Plymouth/Ford quandary all over again. Who can honestly say that one is truly superior to the other two? There is one comforting fact: Replaceable panels generally minimize repair costs.

The most popular superstructure among camping trailers is the all-canvas top. Some experts discount the importance of quality in the fabric,

which makes about as much sense as approving a leaky lifeboat! Exposed to all sorts of weather, folded and refolded, subject to abrasive action as the trailer bounces over rough roads, only high-grade army duck, in 10- to 14-ounce weight, will withstand this abuse.

Canvas tops are mechanically the simplest. Lifting the road cover raises the top into position and extends the bed platforms, this requiring a minimum of musclepower. Another type of canvas top has bed platforms that pull out on roller-bearing slides, automatically lifting the top into place.

A second type has a solid roof, usually of Fiberglas, and canvas sides. These may be operated by a crank mechanism or a manual cantilever system, neither requiring brute strength.

A third type is referred to by its makers as "solid state." Top and sides are of interlocking panels of Fiberglas or plastic. Folded, these units have the characteristic low profile of the canvas top; erect, they resemble a hardtop travel trailer.

At any rate, if it takes you more than five minutes to set up any one of these, you're dawdling.

You have a choice, at this point, of beds that

Camping trailer with rising solid top and fabric sides. TRAIL KING

Apache "solid state" folding trailer. It folds, but all panels are of solid materials, ABS plastic. VESELY

fold or slide out fore and aft—that is, over the *ends* of the trailer box—or in the smaller, more compact units, over the *sides*. With a side fold, the door is at the rear of the trailer; with an over-the-ends style, it's on the curb side. In either case, positioning the beds clears the box for kitchen and lounging room. Incidentally, the beds in most camping trailers are more generous in size than those in travel trailers or truck campers whose inflexible walls limit sleeping space.

During the early 1960s an on-the-ground model was popular. In effect, lifting the top provided a tentlike addition to the end of the trailer, with a sewed-in floor resting directly on the ground. One step up led occupants into the box and its conventional fabric top—a sort of split-level camper. By the late sixties it fell into disuse; then in 1972 it made a comeback with innovations. The product of the Coleman Company, this unit has a solid road cover that swings upward, then down, to rest on the ground, thus providing a bug- and snakeproof floor area in addition to the elevated shelter in the trailer box. This is a compact unit for towing by small cars.

The foregoing are basically the types of camping trailers from which you can make a choice. From this point on, innumerable options are open to you.

All camping trailers provide ample ventilation. Some are equipped with solid, transparent "windows" of flexible plastic that admit daylight but keep out wind and rain. And all include some sort of fabric closure to provide privacy as well as protection from weather. But check to be sure that such window openings can be closed from the inside, and that they do not form pockets that will gather rainwater, to be dumped into the trailer when you open them.

Three-inch-thick foam mattresses are frequently standard, with four-inch foam optional. Bear in mind that these rest on solid plywood or plastic, not on inner springs. Four inches of foam, in this case, are far more comfortable than three.

Camping trailer with bed platforms that fold out over the ends or "fore and aft."
PUMA

Bed platforms on all camping trailers overhang and must be propped. Virtually all models use a 45-degree strut, thrusting the weight of the bed and its occupants against the body of the trailer. A vertical "bedpost" running directly to the ground would be much sturdier but, to my knowledge, is not available. Privacy curtains partition off the beds from the living area and may, or may not, be standard equipment.

The kitchen unit can be one of a hundred combinations. If you're willing to cook and dine outdoors under a canopy, you can get along with a conventional campstove and folding camp table. Or you may choose a stove and dinette suitable for use indoors or out. Even dishwashing can be done outside. After all, tenters do just this. At the other end of the scale, kitchen luxury can match that of the finest travel trailer, with built-ins—an ice box or a refrigerator operating on propane gas, or either 12-volt or 110-volt electricity; a stainless-steel sink with water provided under pressure from a storage tank, or from a campsite hookup. As for

the cooking range, it can be as modern as the one in a high-rise apartment!

For warmth, a portable gas heater is more than ample, but you may also choose a built-in gas furnace with blower and automatic controls. Solid-top trailers can be provided with roof vents. Toilet facilities may also be incorporated, but these are pretty much limited to the portable type, some of which operate on recirculated water from a removable tank and can be flushed up to fifty times before emptying.

Lighting can be portable or built in. A tenter's gasoline lantern will do, but the constant hissing is annoying when brought indoors, and it generates considerable heat, hardly desirable on a warm summer evening, but an asset on a cool night. Portable propane lights, operating from disposable 14-ounce cylinders, are quieter and cooler, but expensive, since cylinders costing $1.50 to $2.00 rarely last more than five to six hours. Hardly classified as luxury, then, are electric dome lights, and outlets into which can be plugged small camper lamps. A converter

This camper has bed platforms that fold out over its sides. NIMROD

makes it possible to use the car's 12-volt battery or the campsite hookup's 110-volt power in the same system.

Manufacturers' brochures portray endless possibilities for inside comfort. In fact, the illustrations are usually somewhat ludicrous. Interior views often lead you to believe that a foreign dignitary is expected for a state dinner in full formal attire. Advertising agencies would do well to portray trailers more realistically, with spaghetti on the tablecloth, kids' toys on the floor, mother's hair in curlers, and father struggling to filet a 12-inch pickerel with a pocketknife at the kitchen sink. This is how camping trailers are really used—not as Saks or Tiffany window displays!

While interior arrangements are more critical to women, the mechanics of the trailer's operation are usually the man's domain. He's more concerned with roadability, and chances are, the tires will first catch his eye. Eight-inch wheels are common on the lighter trailers. Many unhappy users of these claim they are too small and must turn at such high speeds that rubber wears rapidly, blowouts occur, and wheel bearings burn out. It is also said that 8-inch tires are difficult to find for replacement. There's some truth in these claims. Trouble, however, may originate with an axle that may have been bent, even slightly, throwing the wheels and bearings out of line. Abnormal wear results. And, of course, the little tires are not available at every crossroad gasoline station.

On the plus side, many users of 8-inch rubber disclaim any problems with them, and point out that 10- or 12-inch tires are just as difficult to locate. Nevertheless, it makes sense that a larger tire does not rotate at the same rate as a smaller one over a given distance. Properly aligned, wear is bound to be less. Weight of the unit the tire carries is also a factor. Any trailer approaching 1,000 pounds curb weight (weight of the unit and standard equipment but not including occupants or cargo) should be equipped with 10-inch or larger tires. And carry a spare! Optional "continental kits" or spare covers are available in the event you feel that an undecorated tire is an eyesore.

A tongue screw-jack with a dolly wheel is a necessity on any trailer weighing 1,000 pounds or more, and a desirable luxury on lighter models whose tongue weights are hefty. The screw-jack levels the camper when set up; the dolly makes it easier to wheel the unit by hand when necessary. Figuring tongue weight at roughly 10 to 15 per cent of the trailer's weight will indicate to you the need for such a jack.

Leveling jacks are another matter. Many trailers come equipped with only two of these, at the rear corners of the box, so that the trailer has a three-point support. This is usually adequate but less steady than having jacks at all four corners. Some jacks are regular bear traps to operate. Make sure they open and close easily, and adjust for height conveniently.

A trailer's wiring system is often overlooked during the excitement of shopping. Follow the wiring from its coupling with the car's system through the entire unit. Wires hanging loosely underneath, or stapled to exposed areas, will be subject to gravel damage. Loose wiring inside of cupboards and cabinets will snag. Outside wiring should be protected; inside wire should be attached solidly to walls, out of the way.

Decidedly a luxury, but a practical one, is a retractable power cord, much like that on a vacuum cleaner, for tying into a campground outlet. This eliminates coiling and storing an extension.

Clearance lights are a legal requirement, but be sure that they don't merely "cover the law" as to size and effectiveness. They should be clearly visible through fog or heavy rain. And the turn indicators should signal your intentions sharply. Feeble blinkers can be dangerous.

In virtually all states, brakes are mandatory on trailers of 1,000 pounds or more. Electric brakes can be synchronized with the car's braking system, or can be activated separately by the driver. This requires a special installation.

Hydraulic surge brakes are simpler and automatic. A surge controller mounted on the tongue activates the trailer's brakes as a result of forward thrust by the trailer as the car slows. I first saw such brakes on an English Sprite several years ago when it was an impressive novelty. It is still impressive, but no longer novel.

Undercoating is as important to a trailer as to a car, especially if you live near or will travel close to the seacoast, or if you are caught out in a snowstorm when salt is applied to roadways. Without undercoating you run the risk of premature rusting.

A rear bumper of rugged steel is an asset. The chances are that if someone rams you from the rear at speeds greater than five miles per hour, your trailer will be damaged, even with such a bumper, but if you zig when you should

A revived version of the "on the ground" camping trailer and how it is set up. COLEMAN

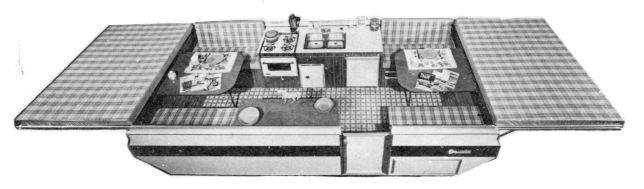

A well-equipped interior, shown with top removed, complete but not lavish. PALOMINO

zag while spotting the camper on your site, the bumper will keep a pine tree from gouging an expensive panel or breaking a tail light.

A folding doorstep is more than a convenience if someone in your family is elderly or physically handicapped. Otherwise you can save a few dollars by stepping a little higher.

The extra niceties are numerous. Awnings over the windows, for example, so that these may be kept open during a rain. A gravel guard, built to withstand the abuse of flying rocks, will protect the front panel. A self-storing screen door is available on all-fabric top models, and a combination storm-and-screen door for solid-top trailers, also self-storing. A large awning provides protection against sun or rain while cooking and dining outside. Fabric walls attached to this transform the area into an extra room. And, instead of the usual single propane tank mounted on the tongue, twin tanks can be installed with an automatic changeover device when one tank runs out.

Among camping trailers, then, the choice ranges from spartan comfort in a simple tent on wheels to town house living.

Chapter 4

TRAVEL TRAILERS

Let's face it: The travel trailer has drawbacks. Its tow car must be specially equipped, and unless it and the trailer are perfectly matched by means of a suitable hitch, sway problems may arise. Sway is a major hazard of trailering in which the unit "fishtails," possibly throwing the tow car out of control. This can be initiated by air displacement when you meet a high-speed bus or large truck on a narrow road or by cross-winds. A trailer more than doubles the over-all length of your vehicle, so that you'll have to allow extra clearance when passing a slower car. Carrying passengers in a trailer is out of the question—in fact, it's illegal in many states. And hearty cussing may evolve when you try to back into an undersized campsite.

These are the negative aspects, but they are overwhelmingly offset by the travel trailer's many advantages. (1) Setting up is easy. Spot the trailer—most modern campgrounds have adequately large campsites or drive-through slots that eliminate the need for backing. Setting up camp consists simply of unlocking the door. Breaking camp is equally simple, except for securing cabinet doors and their contents. (2) The trailer can be left at the campsite, freeing the tow car for other uses. Some campers leave the trailer at a favorite campground on a year-'round basis, using it as a summer cottage. (3) Its use can even be extended through the winter. When winterized it becomes a personal ski lodge or a base camp for snowshoeing, ice fishing, or cross-country skiing. No other recreational vehicle is conveniently that versatile.

As for the perils of sway on the highway, there are effective antisway devices. Driving experience, too, eliminates or minimizes these situations. And you can master backing by borrowing a supermarket parking lot some Sunday morning for a couple of hours. Practice backing into one of the painted parking slots. No campsite is that small!

If you're timid about towing a trailer behind the family car, consider the fact that more than five million recreational vehicles are on the road, with travel trailers outnumbering all other types. What's more, they have an excellent safety record. All in all, if you're at ease behind the wheel of the family car, you can quickly learn to handle a travel trailer.

In fact, towing is easier than choosing from among the numerous types, styles, and sizes. The variety is tremendous! Most popular is the square-profile model, built much like a conventional house with wooden wall studs to which is applied an exterior skin of aluminum or Fiberglas. Interiors are much like those of a dwelling, but on a much smaller scale, of course. This form of construction is the least expensive and provides maximum interior space, especially among the overhead cupboards and cabinets. The "boxy" profile, however, creates some air or wind resistance, and this slightly decreases gas mileage in the tow car, depending upon the size and weight of the trailer.

The streamlined or "aircraft type" trailer has less overhead cabinet space due to the curved contours of the shell, but this is its sole disadvantage. It is stable on the highway and is less susceptible to bus and truck backwash as well as crosswinds. Body construction is sturdier, with aluminum sheets riveted to an aluminum or light steel frame. Such construction is costly, boosting this type of trailer into the "elite" class.

If you're apprehensive about towing a full-sized travel trailer, investigate the telescoping model. When lowered, its profile is much like that of a folded camping trailer. Elevated, it is transformed into a full-headroom unit. Interior facilities are limited slightly but closely approach those of the conventional models. Raising and lowering the upper half is done mechanically and requires no brute strength. Naturally, part of the operating mechanism occupies interior space that cannot otherwise be used. The telescoping trailer can be defined as one step ahead of the camping trailer but not quite as convenient and sophisticated as the travel trailer.

The fifth wheel trailer is designed to be towed by a pick-up truck, the "fifth wheel" being the hitching device resembling that used on highway transport trucks, and located in the body just over, or slightly ahead, of the rear axle. About 25 per cent of the trailer's weight rests on this, as opposed to the 10 or 15 per cent tongue weight of other trailers. This weight placement and the positioning of the hitch lend stability, virtually eliminate sway, and make backing easier. The fifth-wheeler can be detached from the tow truck easily, being equipped with jacks to hold up the front end. Hitching up is simple, since a heavy pin slides into the coupler and is locked into place as the truck is backed under the trailer's overhang. This type of trailer is strictly a highway rig, not intended for rough,

backcountry roads. Severe tilting may damage both the front end of the trailer and the truck body.

Unless you're a structural-steel expert, peering under the trailer to examine its floor frame will prove about as informative as kicking the tires. The frame is all-steel, designed to support a specific trailer. With more than a hundred firms involved in this highly competitive business, none can afford to pass off inadequate underpinnings with any hope of staying in competition.

Springs are another matter. Note their position on the axle. The closer they are to the wheels the better, since a wide support helps cut sway and minimizes lean when the trailer is unevenly loaded—something to be avoided, incidentally. Axles are usually solid, with springs of the leaf type, although some models provide independent wheel suspension. Still others may feature torsion bars.

On heavier trailers, usually those 20 feet or longer, tandem axles and wheels are necessary. "Tandem" means one wheel ahead of the other, as opposed to "dual," wherein two wheels are side by side. The tandem system has advantages. Weight is more widely distributed, and changing a tire is easier.

Don't be impressed by a manufacturer's claim that the hitch weight of his models is unusually low. It should be at least 10 per cent, preferably 12 to 15 per cent, of the trailer's total weight. Weight specifications are shown on a small plaque on the left forward side of the trailer, as required by federal law. "GVW" are important initials. They stand for "gross vehicle weight,"

Standard-type travel trailer, easiest to build and most economical to purchase. TRAVEL-MATE

More luxurious aircraft-type construction trailer, well streamlined. AIRSTREAM

The telescoping trailer with top raised looks much like a conventional travel trailer.
HI-LO

Latest of the recreational vehicles, the fifth-wheel trailer designed for towing with a pick-up truck. WHEEL CAMPER

the weight of the unit plus its cargo. This should never be exceeded by more than a very few pounds. Like wooden canoes and men, travel trailers tend to gain weight with age, as owners keep adding equipment and camping accessories. Excess weight in the aft section will lighten the tongue weight, which may cause sway. Excess weight up forward increases tongue weight. In either case, damage to the trailer's running gear can result. The Recreational Vehicle Institute publishes an enlightening list of typical items put aboard a vacation trailer, with their individual weights, helpful in calculating the GVW. But for an accurate weighing, visit a truck scale. Of this you can be sure: A typical family of four can easily contribute a half ton toward the GVW—food, water, clothing, photo equipment, fishing tackle, guns, outboard motor, books, TV or radio, plus an endless list of other hobby or vacation items. They all add up.

All of which calls for the suggestion that you buy a trailer large enough for your needs. Overloading a small trailer in order to save on initial outlay is poor economy. Buying too large a unit, on the other hand, may afford extra luxury, but it's tantamount to sending a man to do a boy's job; fine if you can afford it.

Describing the interior possibilities of a recreational vehicle, including a travel trailer, is an excercise in superlatives. Short of a sauna bath, no comfort or convenience is impossible—a pressurized water system, water heater, full bath with tub and shower, air conditioning, thermostatically controlled heat, refrigerator with a freezer compartment, modern kitchen range, wall-to-wall shag carpeting, stereo music, closets and cupboards cleverly utilizing all space not devoted to more functional purposes. And, of course, interior decorating done by experts at matching and blending color schemes.

The degree of luxury is governed strictly by your own tastes and means. Stripped down, basic models are available. Or you can go the posh route. Clip a few coupons in trailer magazines and you'll be swamped with colorful and persuasive luxury suggestions. Or visit a dealer's display for a first-hand inspection.

At first you'll be struck by the apparent perfection of the interior design, the compactness of facilities, the clever utilization of space, the doll house effect of miniaturization. Don't, however, accept this as a final appraisal. Allow your first impression to wear off a mite, then, "get tough"! Start appraising objectively.

Flop onto the beds. Are they as comfortable

Tandem wheels help carry larger models, yet tires are easy to change. STEURY

as they look, or do you feel bone-wearying inflexibility of the plywood panels beneath the mattresses? Go through the motions of shaving or taking a shower in the bathroom. Will your elbow tangle with the doorknob as you raise the razor? Will you bump into a towel holder as you step from the shower? Do you have to climb into the lavatory in order to open the door from inside the bath?

Pretend you're doing dishes at the kitchen sink. Will you skin your knuckles on a window closer when reaching for the hot-water faucet? Will the sideboard hold a dish strainer without spilling silverware into the dinette? Are the cupboards located conveniently? Climbing over the kitchen range to put away a saucepan can hardly be termed "convenient"!

Is the "full-sized apartment range" really that, or is it merely a slightly expanded campstove barely able to accommodate a Cub Scout's cook kit?

And the refrigerator. Will it really hold "a full week's supply of food"? Can you reach it conveniently while preparing meals? And here's something easily overlooked: What do you do with kitchen wastes? Can you store soaps, detergents, and dish towels handily?

How about those "luxuriously ample" clothes closets? Will a raincoat and two pair of the kids'

jeans stuff them full? Is there a hamper for soiled clothing, or space in a closet for one? Where will you store the extra gear and clothing, bedding, fishing tackle, cameras?

In appraising a recreational vehicle, remember that you're about to transfer a life-style accustomed to six or more rooms into a single unit quite possibly smaller than your living room. Trailer manufacturers have done wonders in this direction, but be sure that the result fits *your* needs.

Certain basic steps will help:

1. Decide how much you can afford to pay. Prices range from about $800 to upward of $20,000. If you want gold-plated doorknobs, you'll be accommodated.

2. Choose the right size for your family. If your budget is limited and you have two, three, or more children, pass up the luxury-loaded 17-footer in favor of the more spartan, basic 20-footer at about the same price.

3. Learn all you can about travel trailers. The principal sources of information lie in the numerous periodicals.[1] These offer far more currently pertinent data than can be incorporated in any book.

4. Talk to owners about their rigs. Strangers

[1] See the Appendix.

Interiors can be beautiful yet practical. Looking "aft" in a fifth-wheeler. SKAMPER

Looking forward in the same unit. SKAMPER

Compact kitchens are mandatory, but they must also be efficient.
AIRSTREAM

respond enthusiastically when you ask: "How do you like your trailer?" You may learn of advantages you never dreamed of, and on the other hand, a disappointed owner is quick to point out the "bugs" he has encountered.

5. Shop among several dealers. Admit that you're new at the game. Reputable dealers will bend over backward to help, but walk out on the fast-talking smoothie who evades your questions and wants to sign you without delay for "this week's special." It may not be so special next week, once you own it. It may be the last on the lot, a close-out, to be discontinued.

6. Be sure the dealer carries a stock of parts, or has quick access to them, and that he will service the interior appliances without suggesting that you send the defective unit back to the manufacturer, at your expense.

Even with these precautions you may not yet be fully convinced of your choice. In that case, arrange to rent it, or seek a rental agency offering a similar unit. Give it a trial run, at least two or three days, to get the feel of it, and to uncover hidden "bugs." Many dealers will apply all or part of the rental fee toward the purchase price.

A passenger car, fresh off the showroom floor (even after "dealer preparation") cannot adequately tow a trailer weighing 2,000 pounds or more without possible damage to its running gear, suspension, or even to its engine. The car must be "beefed up" for extra duty according to the weight of the trailer and the car's general adaptability to towing.

The dealer can adapt your present car to trailer towing, but ideally the best way to buy a trailer is to buy the tow car at the same time. Necessary accessories can be added at the factory as your car is built at much less cost than in your dealer's service garage. Such installations at the factory are alternative rather than additional installations, so that you pay only the difference between standard and heavy-duty equipment.

Rear axle ratio is vital. This relates to the number of times the engine turns over for each revolution of the rear wheels. The engine and the gear ratio must be matched suitably for towing. Car manufacturers have specific recommendations for their various models.

Automatic transmissions have surpassed manual shifting by a wide margin for trailer use. Not only is driving easier and smoother, but wear on the running gear is minimized. Manual transmissions can be used, of course, but they require a heavy-duty clutch and a four-speed range. For towing large trailers with an automatic shifting mechanism, a transmission-oil cooler should be installed.

Gear ratios for trailer towing call for faster-turning engines. This requires additional cooling capacity, which is provided by an oversized radiator, and sometimes by a fan shroud to concentrate the full flow of cool air over the engine block. And in case of overheating and subsequent boilover, a reservoir catches the boiling coolant, which would otherwise escape via the overflow tube. The coolant is then fed back into the radiator.

Since you'll require electric power for two units—trailer and car—an oversized generator or alternator is virtually mandatory. Consider that you may have a second battery in the trailer, plus double the number of tail, directional, and clearance lights, in addition to interior lights and accessories. The standard generator or alternator can't handle this load satisfactorily. For electrical service from the car to the trailer, a special wiring harness is installed, the connection made at the hitch by means of two plugs.

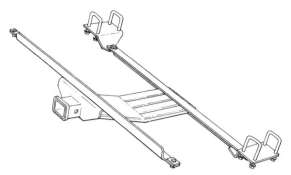

A Class II hitch. EAZ-LIFT

At this writing Detroit is still resisting a growing demand for a crankcase-oil cooler for cars towing heavier trailers, those requiring Class III or equalizer hitches. Dick Morch, test driver for *Trailer Travel* magazine,[2] has been urging this as a result of his road tests. A crankcase-oil cooler differs from one designed to cool transmission oil, although one "add on" model currently available handles both chores.

It stands to reason that when you add two hundred or more pounds at the tow car's rear bumper (tongue weight), this will tilt the car's front end upward. Heavy-duty suspension systems counter this, including variable air-pressure shock absorbers, which can be "inflated" when you check your tire pressures.

Power steering is not an absolute necessity

[2] See the Appendix.

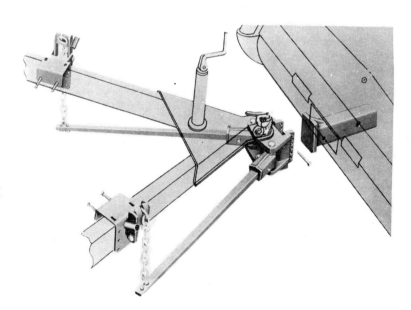

Equalizer hitch thrusts weight to forward end of tow car, eliminating "tail drag." VALLEY TOW-RITE

A sway-control equalizer hitch eliminates most trailer-hauling road problems. EAZ-LIFT

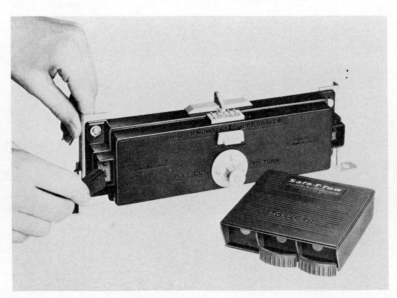

Automatic sway control applies trailer's brakes automatically should sway develop. Its reaction is faster than that of the driver. SAFE-T-TOW

when rolling along on the open highway, but in heavy traffic or while maneuvering the trailer into a campsite, you'll bless this power assist.

The brakes on a given vehicle are designed to stop it quickly and safely. But add a trailer weighing as much as the car, and you double the thrust or burden on the brakes. An almost new braking system must be adapted to the rig. This should start with power front disk brakes, which resist "fading" and help keep the vehicle from swerving during a panic stop. But the trailer needs brakes, too. Surge brakes, already mentioned, may be used, or you may choose electric brakes, which can be synchronized with those of the tow car.

Since conventional rear-view mirrors have their views blocked by a trailer, "long horns" are necessary, extending far enough to each side of the towing vehicle to "see around" the trailer. These generally are removable, or may be folded back out of the way when not needed. If a trailer is not in tow, some states require this as protection for in-town jaywalkers!

The most important accessory of all, however, is the trailer hitch. A Class I hitch is a simple unit bolted to the extreme rear of the tow car by as few as four bolts, and is suited to trailers whose gross weight does not exceed 2,000 pounds or create hitch weights of over 200. Despite its seeming capacity to handle substantial tongue weight, the Class I hitch is generally unsuitable for travel trailers. A Class II hitch is only slightly more difficult to install and costs just a bit more,

but it will handle trailers up to 3,500 pounds or tongue weights up to 300.

Beyond these weights a Class III or equalizer hitch is called for. In essence, this hitch is designed to lift some of the burden from the tow car's rear suspension system by thrusting some of the weight forward to the car's front end and back to the trailer's running gear. By means of spring bars, this type of hitch keeps both the trailer and the car on an even keel. It is suitable for trailers up to 6,000 to 7,000 pounds. Heavier trailers are usually too much for passenger cars and are best hauled by light trucks or truck-framed station wagons.

Some load-equalizer hitches incorporate sway controls. Such controls may also be added. By means of tension bars or cables, a trailer's tendency to fishtail is inhibited. Another type of sway control[3] is a braking device that operates automatically whenever the trailer starts to swerve even slightly. A simple device installed at the rear of the tow car, it applies the trailer brakes even before the driver can react, sometimes even before he is aware that sway has started!

Major car manufacturers all publish highly informative booklets covering trailer towing and necessary tow-car accessories. This is a highly technical subject, but such pamphlets are written for laymen. You won't need a degree from MIT to grasp the wealth of information they contain!

[3] Safe-T-Tow. See the Appendix.

Chapter 5

TRUCK CAMPERS

The first truck camper I ever saw was owned by a visiting fisherman whom we guides had dubbed "The Shelldrake," after the merganser duck, a notorious gobbler of small trout. The angler wasn't popular among owners of rental cabins in the area, and as for the guides, they would gladly have dropped a 6o-foot spruce across the plywood box on the back of the pick-up truck in which the Shelldrake slept. Naturally he hadn't hired a cabin. He had his own boat, hauled atop his rig. He'd brought in his own supplies. We might have forgiven his not spending any money among us, but not the fact that he was always first to wet a line in the best fishing pools. We guides went back to camp every night with our sportsmen and each morning returned to the fishing grounds. The Shelldrake was always there when we arrived. He'd camped by the stream in his rig. Luckily for him, he stayed only a few days, possibly sensing that there was a move afoot to push his camper down over the brink of Slidedown Gulch.

The Shelldrake was trying to tell us something more than twenty-five years ago. With a truck camper, almost any 10′×20′ area can be a campsite. Truck power combined with high road clearance opens up rough roads impassable to passenger-type vehicles, yet passengers may ride safely in the camper. And, at the same time that a truck/camper combination is usually much less costly than a passenger car and a travel trailer, the truck camper is more highly maneuverable on the highway and off the road.

There's a certain "maleness" about a truck camper—it brings to mind the hunter or fisher-man—but this does not rule out its use by a small family, and certainly it is a favorite rig among couples.

Women sometimes need reassurance that a truck can be a respectable vacation vehicle. The barren interior of twenty years ago is automotive history. The hard seat, the minimal conveniences, the stiff springs, engine noise—all of these are gone. The interior of today's pick-ups are downright posh—designed, I suspect, by lady interior decorators. Color, convenience, and comfort are standard. As for riding qualities, the pick-up won't match those of the limousine hired for society weddings, but it offers a far better ride than I've had in some New York or Chicago taxis!

Pick-ups are rated according to their basic carrying capacities: one-half, three-quarter, or one ton. Obviously these are inadequate for toting campers. So they are "beefed up," just as an automobile is modified to tow a heavy travel trailer. A half-ton truck can be equipped to carry a full ton; a three-quarter ton unit, up to two tons; and a one-ton truck, close to three tons! Truck bodies (the cargo space) range from 6′ to 8′ long.

As with the travel trailer and tow car, the ideal approach is to purchase a truck to match the camper you have in mind. The truck can then be factory-equipped for its chores, at a saving to you. On the other hand, if you already own a truck, your choice of camper will be limited to the vehicle's ability to carry it, possibly after some modifications by a local dealer.

Among the camper units, the so-called "slide-

"Slide-in" camper is an integral part of truck during travel, yet can be removed. STEURY

in" is the most popular, possibly because of the tremendous variety of models available and its general adaptability to virtually all pick-up trucks. The floor area is usually that of the truck body, 6' to 8' long—although 10-footers or longer are mounted with a moderate overhang at the stern. A "cab-over" is usually standard. This is a projection over the truck cab in which is located the "master bedroom," a full-sized double-bed. The term "slide-in" is a slight misnomer. It is generally lowered into the truck body by means of a set of jacks, although a few versions can be rolled into the body. Once in place, "tie-downs" attach the camper to the truck.

The obvious advantage of this is that the camper can be removed between trips, freeing the vehicle for humbler chores. Few users, however, demount their campers at a campsite. Removing the unit is not *that* simple a procedure. Another advantage of this type of rig is that a boat or utility trailer can be towed; hence the truck camper's popularity among sportsmen.

The chassis-mount camper is more spacious. It is attached directly, and permanently, to the truck's chassis or frame, the cargo body having been omitted. Such units run to 14 or 15 feet long and may be mounted on trucks having a longer wheelbase than the conventional pick-up. A cab-over is invariably included. Essentially this type of camper is a travel trailer without wheels, mounted on a truck. The interior most closely approximates that of a travel trailer, including the convenience of a curbside entry. Some models provide direct access from the cab.

The telescoping camper comes close to fulfilling automobile makers' silly claims of "small car; big, roomy interior." The camper is small since the upper half is lowered mechanically to provide a low profile during travel. And it has a "big, roomy interior" when the top is raised for occupancy, including full headroom. This type of camper is more than a gadget. The telescoping feature allows it to slip under overhead limbs that brush, and sometimes damage, slide-ins or chassis mounts during travel on back roads. Some models may even be driven into a garage, but I doubt that this is a prime reason for their increasing popularity. Compactness on the road, reduced wind or air resistance, minimal sway or lean—

An 11-foot slide-in camper approximates interior convenience of medium-sized travel trailer. CORSAIR

these are more legitimate reasons. Even with models having a cab-over, some sacrifice in convenience is necessary, of course. Most users of this type are concerned primarily with a basic, convertible shelter on wheels.

The same philosophy accompanies the choice of a "shell" camper, this being little more than a cover over the cargo area, its height equal to that of the cab, or possibly 12 to 18 inches above this. Full headroom is not possible, of course. The tailgate is replaced by a rear section that includes a miniature door, and side windows provide daytime lighting.

Cost is relatively low, and it serves as a superb "base camp" for fishermen, hunters, backpackers, climbers, and other outdoorsmen to whom a wheeled-camper is a means of transportation combined with simple shelter. With its "low overhead" it is challenged on rough, brushy roads only by the telescoping model.

For the ultimate in stylish camping, however, top honors must go to the chassis-mount camper. Any accessory or appliance that can be built into a travel trailer of medium size can be incorporated into a chassis-mount camper, and usually is! Since these interior possibilities were

A chassis-mount truck camper is permanently attached, provides much greater interior living space. DEL REY

Telescoping truck camper lowers profile for travel, provides comfortable headroom on the campground. SKAMPER

detailed in the previous chapter, there is no need to repeat them here, except to point out that such ultraposh furbishings as a full bath are usually omitted. A shower, yes—but a full bath is stretching the luxury motif a mite.

The slide-in camper is somewhat more limited. While all of the necessities, and some luxuries, may be included, these will generally be more compact, even miniaturized to some degree. The kitchen sink, for instance, will be smaller; the dinette a far cry from a dining room table; and living space generally restricted. But then, all camping units, whether tents or wheeled vehicles, are compromises. A careful choice from among numerous truck camper floor plans will provide for your needs, and even some of your inclinations toward the posh.

In the telescoping model, interior appliances and convenience features must conform to the constricting effects of lowering the top for travel. But this need not mean spartan discomfort—witness the interiors of the more luxurious camping trailers.

In buying a ready-to-go camper, whether chassis-mount, slide-in, or telescoping, follow the suggestions made in the previous chapter with regard to travel trailers. "Try out" the unit by going through the motions of living in it for at least a half hour. Better yet, rent it for a weekend.

The shell camper needs no such in-depth appraisal, since most users build in their own interiors. Personal ingenuity and self-expression can be given reign here—a bunk or two, a small table, cabinet, possibly a vented heater, and electric lights. Bottled gas can be hooked up to a cookstove and refrigerator, although most truck-shell campers use a simple camper's ice chest. Stoves, too, are generally portable rather than built-in, so that they can be used outside, this also true of a folding table and chairs. Adding a canvas canopy to the rear of the camper provides shade on a hot day, and protection from rain, too. Interior racks for fishing tackle or hunting rifles are possibilities, also. Whatever you build into your truck shell, make provisions for battening down all loose equipment; otherwise these will be tossed about while you're negotiating a rough or "washboardy" road!

According to most manufacturers' specifications, all truck campers fall into the "large, economy size" category. Invariably sleeping capacity is overrated. It is a rare dinette, for example, that converts into a "spacious double bed." And quite possibly you can bunk three or four youngsters in the large cab-over bed if you can convince them to sleep rather than play "king of the hill"! What I'm trying to say is that a truck camper is ideally suited to a couple. Beyond that number of occupants, the necessity for com-

Every cubic foot of a truck camper's interior must serve a purpose, as this one does.
COACHMAN

promise progresses alarmingly. With crowding, patience wears thin. A well-disciplined family can enjoy a truck camper through the organization of routine activities, but vacation chaos can result if the camper's space limitations are disregarded. There is no rule of thumb. Whether or not a truck camper is the best choice for your family only you can decide.

If I seem to have propounded a somewhat negative attitude, it is only because most camping writers describe tents, wheeled campers, and other equipment strictly in glowing terms, as if fearful of offending advertisers, or risking their discount privileges, in either case doing a rank disservice to readers. No item of camping gear has yet attained ultimate perfection. Shortcomings exist, and these should be pointed out.

If you have appraised the truck camper objectively and then decided to buy one, the chances are you have made a good choice. Your next move is toward a truck to carry it. If you've chosen a simple shell, a vehicle fresh off the showroom floor without "extras" will probably handle it nicely. For a telescoping camper, minor modifications of the truck and its running gear may be required. But if your decision is in favor of a slide-in or a chassis mount, the truck must be matched to the camper.

Either of these campers is bulky; hence wind or air resistance places an added burden on the power plant and the running gear. The camper's weight is usually greater than the rated capacity of a "stock" or standard truck. This applies stress to the power train, too, and also to the suspension system. Also affecting this is the raised center of gravity. But put aside fears that you'll add the straw that breaks the pick-up truck's chassis! Truck makers have adapted their vehicles and designed options that can more than double rated carrying capacity.

Beefing up a truck to carry a camper is somewhat like modifying a passenger car to pull a trailer, except that the truck must *carry* the load, not tow it. Wind resistance and weight—especially in hilly country—call for ample power under the hood, up to a 450-cubic-inch V-8 engine, this matched to a suitable axle ratio—4.10 to 1, for example. For smaller campers a 307-to-350-cubic-inch V-8 with an axle ratio of 3.40 or 3.07 to 1 may be more than adequate.

Obviously, weight affects the suspension system as well as the power plant. Add to this the camper's high center of gravity and its susceptibility to strong crosswinds, plus its tendency to lean to the outside on a curve. These point to the need for heavy duty and/or auxiliary rear springs, super shock absorbers, and front and rear stabilizer bars. In addition to these special underpinnings, hydraulic shock absorbers (not to be confused with the axle type) can be rigged between the camper and the truck, these attached between the cab-over and the cab, and within the truck body. These regulate flexing, which is inevitable, even desirable, between the truck and the camper. Without this flexibility, damage could result in the tie-down system.

For heavier campers, up to almost three tons, carried on one-ton-rated trucks, dual wheels are in order. Their ability to support heavy loads is obvious, and they also offer greater traction on and off the road. Unsurfaced back roads are usually a combination of rocky outcroppings, potholes, ruts, and mudholes. Here dual wheels perform superbly.

Other equipment—standard or optional—includes a coolant reservoir system, heavy-duty radiator, and a special wiring harness. "Long horn" rear-view mirrors are necessary on trucks carrying slide-ins or chassis mounts.

Weight distribution is vital to roadability. Like other vehicles, the truck camper has a designated gross vehicle weight, usually indicated on the inside of the glove compartment door. This is the total weight of the truck, the camper, its cargo, and its passengers. But there's more to

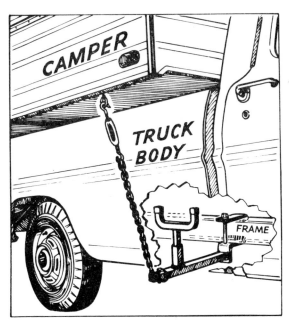

This type of tie-down for truck campers stabilizes unit for highway travel. CAMPER-CLAMPER

The recreational vehicle weight watcher's guide. DODGE

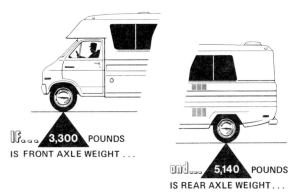

RV WEIGHT WATCHER'S GUIDE

IF... **3,300** POUNDS IS FRONT AXLE WEIGHT ...

and... **5,140** POUNDS IS REAR AXLE WEIGHT...

THE COMBINED FRONT AND REAR AXLE WEIGHTS CANNOT EXCEED THE GROSS VEHICLE WEIGHT.

GVW IS **7,700** POUNDS ....

consider. Gross *axle* weight is equally important, and this too is shown on the plaque in the glove compartment. It is possible to stay within the truck's gross vehicle weight yet place unreasonable stress on the front or rear end by poor weight distribution. The most common tendency is to overload the rear axle.

Weighty equipment such as outboard motors should be stored well ahead of the rear axle. It may be a wise move to rig the spare tire, or carry a trail bike on the front bumper rather than at the rear. Excessive weight at the stern can be dangerous—sway may develop, and steering may be difficult. Such a condition is usually obvious—the front end tilts upward. If your truck and camper are properly matched and suitably loaded, it will ride on an even keel. If there is any doubt about this, visit a truck scale. Weigh the front and rear axles, as well as the over-all vehicle. Under no circumstances should the combined axle weights exceed the gross vehicle weight.

Another weight aspect sometimes overlooked is the placement of incidental cargo—canned foods, for example. Keep all heavy goods close to the floor. This lowers the center of gravity and decreases the tendency toward lean or sway. Balance your load from side to side, too.

NOTE: Major truck manufacturers, notably General Motors, Ford, and Chrysler annually issue detailed literature regarding their trucks and available modifications for truck campers. The same is true regarding tow cars for trailers. Albeit their aim is to sell their products, their publications are far more detailed than any book such as this one can be. Of necessity I have pointed out only the general requirements of trucks and tow cars. The specifics should be obtained from manufacturers' publications. Recreational vehicle dealers can also be helpful.

Chapter 6

MOTOR HOMES—MINI, MEDIUM, AND MAMMOTH

Westward-bound covered wagons were probably the first American sleep-aboard campers. Motorized versions go back many years, too—at least to 1923, possibly earlier. A Model T Ford of that vintage, rigged as a fold-out camper, is the oldest I've seen, but don't conclude from this that I probably voted for Woodrow Wilson or Warren G. Harding. I first saw this unit, a beautifully restored museum piece, only five years ago. However, I must admit that the Model A featured in my life.

Mine was a 1931 used roadster purchased in 1935 for $175. Gas was $.19 a gallon; *Lulubelle* delivered 19 miles per gallon. For a penny a mile I probed New Hampshire's backcountry in search of trout streams. But I soon discovered that my daily quest for a tentsite, plus the pitching and breaking of my camp, detracted seriously from my allotted span of weekend fishing time. I needed greater mobility; more fishing, less camping.

So I rigged the roadster as a camper. By day I carried a contrived folding bed platform in the rumble seat, along with a rolled cot mattress and a $6.00 kapok sleeping bag. Come night, I removed the front seat and extended the bed so that I could sleep aboard, my head near the dashboard, my feet in the rumble seat. Under a mosquito netting large enough to drape over the entire car, I was secure as a clam at high tide. Pitching or breaking camp took just four minutes, rarely interfering with the evening rise!

None of today's motor homes can guarantee you the superb trout fishing that *Lulubelle* led

me to, but the economy with which she carried me through the countryside can almost be matched by some of the current minihomes.

These are best exemplified by the thousands of Volkswagen buses on the road, with interiors converted by their owners—folding bunks, improvised kitchens, dining tables, even curtains on the windows. Such simple conversions add only a few dollars to the over-all price of the car, yet provide the flexibility and economy required by a budget-conscious family on vacation or on weekend jaunts.

More sophisticated comforts and conveniences are often added by a handyman who is adept with tools. Some seek to avoid that "homemade" look by using professionally drawn plans and ready-made kits offered by firms advertising in recreational vehicle magazines.[1]

Commercial conversions set a fast pace for ingenuity, not only with the Volkswagen but also in adapting the roomier Dodge, Ford, and Chevrolet vans; the facilities and decor built into these relatively small vehicles are truly astounding. Standard equipment frequently includes a one-piece molded Fiberglas bathroom fitted with a shower head, lavatory, and marine-type toilet; water storage and sanitary holding tanks; 110-volt to 12-volt converter; nylon pile or indoor/outdoor carpeting; a kitchen comparable to that in a fine travel trailer, though necessarily more compact; professionally decorated interior, plus of course, the taken-for-granted disappearing

[1] See the Appendix for a list of these.

bunks, folding tables, armchair-type seating, and the nook-and-cranny cupboards. Full headroom is achieved by means of a permanent or retractable raised roof.

"Options" are available, too—air conditioning, stereo music, TV antenna, stove hood with exhaust fan, electric generator, and a myriad other luxuries which, as the auction ads say, are "too numerous to mention." And all of this in a vehicle barely 17 feet long, bumper to bumper! This posh highway cabin crusier will, however, cost upward of $6,000.

The true minihome or "chopped van" is not necessarily more luxurious, but it is more spacious. This is not a conversion but rather a specially built camper attached to a bare chassis with only the driver's cab in place. The camper somewhat resembles a cab-over travel trailer without wheels. It is not, of course.

Full headroom is attained without a "bubble top"; floor space is greater, since it may extend to full legal highway width; and additional sleeping quarters are built into the cab-over. Interiors can be, and usually are, as lavish as design ingenuity can make them, rivaling on a smaller scale those of the finest travel trailers. Price, of course, goes up accordingly.

The true, full-size motor home is built on a bare chassis minus any sort of cab or body. Most popular among these are the medium-priced— $7,000 to $10,000—rigs ranging from 20 to 25 feet in length. Generally, these units combine spaciousness, practicality, comfort, and convenience with only a touch of elegance. They are rarely lavish since, in this price range in a highly competitive market, manufacturers seek to offer a relatively large machine at a "popular" price. Along with spaciousness, they must, of course, provide basic motor home gracious living: comfortable beds, a complete and convenient kitchen, bath with at least a shower, adequate closets, some sort of a music system—usually radio and tape deck with multispeakers, water heater, thermostatically controlled heat, even air conditioning. Add to this the motor home manufacturer's cost for the chassis and power plant. Obviously, there's little margin left for a sumptuous interior. Not that the decor in this class of motor home is spartan—it is usually very attractive—but don't look for expensive drapes or gold-threaded upholstery.

A good rule of thumb when buying a medium-priced motor home is to buy the least lavishly furnished model within a given price range and size. If brand A, at $10,000, has an interior like a Hollywood version of a sultan's palace, while

Raising the roof (at left) or attaching a permanent "bubble" provides headroom in economical van campers. TURTLE TOP

brand B, at the same price, reminds you of a first-class motel room, buy brand B. Its builder has put his cost into suitable running gear, quality appliances, and sturdy framing. Motor home builders who skimped on framing, on appliances, and on running gear, went out of business years ago. As with travel trailers and truck campers, look for the seal of the Recreational Vehicle Institute.

Of course, if you can afford to move into ultraelegance on wheels, the 25-to-32-footers, and longer, start at about $16,000 and up—often way up! What were expensive options in the medium-priced rigs are standard equipment aboard these sumptuous land yachts. Describing posh interiors in recreational vehicles makes for monotonous reading. But when a motor home has a built-in vacuum cleaner system, automatic dishwasher, and a bath salts dispenser, it has arrived at ultimate luxury on wheels.

These are the playthings of movie stars, TV personalities who want to rough it while on location, board chairmen and company presidents on expense accounts, none of whom is about to consult a book such as this for advice in buying a motor home.

Also in this upper-bracket category is the custom-converted intercity bus. Greyhound and Continental Trailways, for example, offer used buses for sale as they are removed from highway service.[2] In terms of mileage, they have been around the world several times, but they are still highly serviceable as private coaches. Stripped of seats, prices for these start at about $10,000. A set of used tires, about $750; a new set, $1,500 or more. Conversion of such buses is usually done by firms specializing in this work, often guided by interior designs planned by their customers. In 1972 I was invited aboard after such a conversion, but despite the graciousness of my hosts, I was uncomfortable. The rig had cost $108,000!

Among the less affluent, discarded school buses are favorites for conversion, their interiors definitely boasting a "homemade" motif, but I doubt that the families aboard these have any less fun on the road than the folks driving a former New York-to-Chicago express bus, now a rolling mansion. Since I'm completely baffled by any machinery having more than two moving

Another version of the expandable roof for vans, again combining economy with comfort. SPORTSMOBILE

parts, I stand in awe of anyone who can restore to highway use a worn-out school bus and keep it running. Such conversions are strictly for the mechanically adept.

"Motor coaching" has developed a unique camaraderie that has evolved into the Family Motor Coach Association.[3] It publishes its own colorful magazine, along with a directory of suppliers of appliances and components for conversions of all types. Membership is open to any motor home owner, whether his rig is a highway, urban, or school bus conversion, or a prebuilt commercial model.

Neither the $108,000 Greyhound conversion nor the $400 beat-up school bus now a family camper is typical, however. The average American buys a rig on the upper side of the medium price range. It's a matter of record that manufacturers attempting to market "low price" or

---

2 See the Appendix.

3 See the Appendix.

The "chopped van" manages reasonable gas consumption with spaciousness. COACHMAN

Ultracomfort, as the author road tests a Grumman 21-foot motor home. ELEANOR RIVIERE

"utility" vehicles have had to withdraw these from the salesrooms. They simply have not sold.

The trick to keeping within one's financial limits is to evaluate the "options" objectively. Otherwise you may be in line for a luxurious ride to the poorhouse! How much true vacation pleasure will you derive from a "color coded" 5-foot bathtub at $389 extra? Is a 40-gallon holding tank really worth $55 more than a 30-gallon model? A medicine cabinet, barely large enough to hold the aspirin you'll need on payment day, at $32.47? Or a road flare kit for $27.88?

Before starting to shop seriously, decide how much you can afford for an over-all price, and if the rig is to be financed, what the monthly budget will stand. And stick to these figures. Beware of "easy, on-the-spot" financing. It may prove expensive. You can very likely obtain a more favorable interest rate from your own bank.

Touring in a motor home, even with overnight stops in a campground, cannot by any elasticity of imagination be called "camping." Rolling about the country in such style cannot

What the "underpinnings" look like in a well-built motor home. Bolted and welded I-beams insure a solid foundation. HARVEST

be likened to sleeping under canvas and cooking over an open fire. Nor should it be. The motor home stands on its own merits.

Our first experience was aboard a 22-foot Winnebago. A half-hour briefing by the dealer and we were on our way, headed for Cape Cod. Provincetown's narrow streets are tricky, but power steering eased us around nicely. Then, lunch aboard at Cape Cod National Seashore and a long walk on the beach. The next day we drove *Big Winnie* 250 years back into history, touring Plymouth, visiting the old burial ground, boarding the *Mayflower II,* then out to restored Plimoth Village. Then we decided to dine out. Grimy by then, I put a nickel in the meter where we'd stopped on Plymouth's main street, while Eleanor drew the curtains. With street traffic on one side, pedestrians on the other, we showered and dressed. The dinner, a block away, was superb.

A few days later we rolled into Dolly Copp Campground in the White Mountain National Forest, where my son Bill, and his wife, Lee, joined us. In fact, they temporarily abandoned their camping trailer, moving in with us. Bill and I climbed Mount Washington via the Tuckerman Trail over the Headwall. Base "camp" that night was again *Big Winnie,* her luxurious beds soothing my tortured muscles. Then on to Vermont for a stop at the famed Orvis fishing tackle plant in Manchester, stops at country stores and antique shops, and several overnight pauses in various campgrounds of the Green Mountain National Forest, where the program

Wall and roof construction details of a well-assembled road camper.
CHAMPION

Looking "astern" in a well-designed motor home interior. COACHMAN

Looking forward in another interior. Bed at right is a quickly converted dinette.
SKAMPER

ranged from a steak cookout to feeding raccoons that came into the campsite to sniff the big tires! Only a few weeks ago, Eleanor and I enjoyed a Maine jaunt aboard a Grumman 21-footer, the trip equally as delightful as that in *Big Winnie.*

I drove logging trucks during my early days in the woods, so the size and bulk of motor homes posed no clearance problems for me. I learned long ago to "swing wide," for example, to avoid climbing curbstones or short-cutting sharp curves. However, even a driver accustomed only to a small car soon gets the feel of these big vehicles. As for handling in highway traffic, I found myself cruising at 60 miles per hour on Massachusetts' infamous Route 128 with unconscious ease. (This was *before* the gas crisis!)

Daily gas stops may run you what at first glance may seem to be a horrendous amount for fuel, but is actually less than the price of a half-way decent motel room. Food costs vary little from those at home. Campground fees are slightly higher for luxury rigs, of course, because of utility hookups.

However, depreciation should be considered. Even if you paid $25,000 for your rig, it will eventually wear out. Depreciation experience is still sketchy, so no rule of thumb exists yet. But as used motor homes begin to appear in increasing numbers on dealers' lots, depreciation patterns will become apparent, probably paralleling those of automobiles.

Motor homes have one major disadvantage. Going into town for an overlooked pound of bacon means driving an 8-mile-per-gallon rig for local errands. Careful planning while shopping can eliminate these expensive oversights. Some motor home owners get around this problem by towing a small car, or carrying a motor bike or ten-speed bicycle on a bumper rack.

The problem of where to empty the holding tank is fast being alleviated as campgrounds, service stations, and recreational vehicle dealers install sanitary stations in rapidly increasing numbers. Several directories listing such stations are published.[4]

Motor home advertisers—and this is true of travel trailer manufacturers, too—frequently portray their rigs poised by a mountain lake, snow-capped peaks in the distance, deer in the fore-

The author tinkers his son Bill's pack, as the two prepare to leave their "base camp" for an assault on Mount Washington. ELEANOR RIVIERE

ground. "The wilderness is yours," they proclaim. This is bilge wash! The motor home and the travel trailer are hardly wilderness vehicles. With deft handling you might negotiate a twisting, rutted back road, but the motor home is not designed for this sort of travel. What's more, where you can travel, others can follow, even precede you. If you want to get away from it all, buy a canoe or backpack, not a motor home.

Much of the technical data referred to earlier with regard to travel trailers and truck campers applies to motor homes. You won't have to match the load to the running gear. Engineers have done this for you. But it is still vital that you observe the weight limitations designated on the plaque you'll find up near the driver's seat. Maximum gross vehicle weight and maximum gross axle weight should be adhered to.

Motor home travel is not camping, but whatever it is, it's delightful!

[4] See the Appendix.

Chapter 7

THE CAMPFIRE

Too many of us are "conclusion jumpers"—especially true of the current crop of instant environmentalists who have not done their homework and who unalterably adopt or oppose any cause after a cursory glance at a smidgen of evidence. Facts are never permitted to cloud the issue! The extremists would outlaw snowmobiles, trail bikes, hunting, outboard motors, travel trailers, even campfires!

In my last book, *Backcountry Camping*,[1] I described the comfort and companionship of a night fire before my open tent. Writing in the first issue of the superb magazine *Backpacker* (Vol. 1, No. 1, Spring 1973), its book review editor wrote, ". . . while Riviere enjoys the luxury of a sleep fire, the wilderness gets pushed back a little further." The editor tossed in such jibes as "19th-century hatchetman" and "land-development trainee" for good measure. Frankly, I chuckled all the way to the woodpile because, in the areas where I build campfires, the forest around me grows more wood in one day than my campfires consume in a month!

Snap judgments by unknowing "experts" always result in misguided generalizations. Of course, fires must be limited or banned in areas of overuse—Cape Cod, parts of the Adirondacks, the Appalachian Trail, the High Sierras, and probably dozens of other high-use recreational regions. And certainly foraging for firewood in crowded state parks is out of the question. "Pushing back the wilderness" occurs on the fringe of busy campgrounds and along hiking trails where there's a summer-long rush hour. But in the Maine woods, in Quebec, Ontario, or British Columbia? Here, waste tops and slash from logging operations alone would supply ten thousand campers with firewood for a hundred years! Blanket condemnation of the campfire makes no sense. A cheery blaze is not necessarily an ecological sin.

For instance, at my camp deep in the Maine woods, I annually cut down several red maples. These grow tall and spindly, are relatively short-lived, have little commercial value, and invariably suffer from heart rot long before they're fifty feet high. When seasoned, however, red maple is pretty fair firewood. It keeps my camp warm during the chilly nights of October and November. As a bonus when I cut these down, the sunshine is able to reach the forest floor, pouring life into thousands of tiny balsam firs. That's helping Mother Nature, not fooling her!

As for the sometimes-heard ludicrous cry of "air pollution" from campfire smoke, this is the utter height of the ridiculous! All of the campfires in the national parks on any given day are less harmful to the atmosphere than a single industrial smokestack. In fact, "the only penalty inflicted upon the environment by prescribed burning (of firewood) is a small and temporary decrease in visibility."[2]

Few of us can resist the hypnotism of a campfire, probably because there is still in us the

[1] Garden City, N.Y.: Doubleday & Company (1971).

[2] J. Alfred Hall, *Forest Fuels: Prescribed Fire and Air Quality* (Portland, Oreg.: Pacific Northwest Forest and Range Experiment Station, U. S. Forest Service, 1972).

urge of primitive man to seek the warmth, light, and reassurance of the flames' glow. The ring of firelight draws us irresistibly, and which of us, watching the Devil Dance of the flames, has not imagined seeing strange forms writhing in the fire—faces, animals, objects—fluttering momentarily, but clearly, then disappearing? The campground without a campfire is a desolate place, for who ever heard of campers sitting around a gasoline stove, watching its regimented flame, popping corn, or swapping yarns while the moon sweeps overhead just shy of the stars? Granted, campers can live without a campfire, and some do, but the experience isn't a full one.

The campfire isn't entirely a romantic luxury, however. The comparatively few family campers who prepare meals over an open fire have learned that no camp stove can match the speed and efficiency of an open flame when it comes to cooking. Also, when there is soggy clothing to be dried, a wood fire has no peer.

Having at one time been a fire warden, I'm convinced that campers are sometimes blamed for forest fires when more diligent investigation might have proved the culprit to have been a careless woods worker.

Nevertheless, caution is necessary. Even in a well-designed campground fireplace, it's not safe to leave a blaze unattended. If the wind is blowing or if woodlands are particularly dry, it becomes downright foolhardy to leave the fire alone. Although many of today's so-called "forest fires" are really brush or grass fires that burn over what foresters call "junk lands," these fires can spread into valuable timber or engulf buildings. Children playing with matches is one of the leading causes of such fires. If there are youngsters in the family who show an interest in fire building, this should be encouraged *under guidance*. Allow *them* to build the campfire—in the fireplace, showing them the need for safety and caution. Smokers probably have the poorest safety record with regard to outdoor fires. Cigarette and cigar butts, as well as pipe dottle, should be deposited in the campsite fireplace, not on the ground. If you're away from your site, or walking in the woods, drop these into puddles and streams or grind them underfoot into bare soil or on a rock. Better yet, don't smoke while walking in dry woodlands.

In park campgrounds and in commercial camping areas, foraging for firewood is usually forbidden. Fuel wood is therefore often provided at a small charge. This may take on strange forms—old bridge timbers, boards from demolished buildings, sawmill slabs or edgings, or even woodturning-mill wastes. Generally such firewood is cut to length but not split. That's up to the camper.

On family campgrounds the knowledge of firewood characteristics has lost much of its significance. The woodpile may include anything from explosive pitch pine to soggy sassafras. Family campers can get along with the knowledge that softwoods make the best tinders and kindling. These are the evergreens, such as pine, spruce, fir, and hemlock. The hardwoods, in most instances, are the deciduous trees (they lose their leaves in the fall), and these are heavier and closer-grained than softwoods. They are better fuels for longer-lasting fires. Not only do they burn longer, but they're less likely to throw sparks, and most leave a bed of glowing coals.

Because firewoods provided on family campgrounds are not always the best-suited species, fire-building technique takes on a new importance. Much romantic gibberish has appeared in camping literature, particularly in the description of the several types of fires that can be built, including such idiotic nonsense as the Teepee, Log Cabin, Hunter's, and Lazy Man's fires. Most of these are impractical fallacies. The Teepee will tumble and scatter the infant flames. The Log Cabin burns out its innards and leaves smoldering walls. The Hunter's fire entails an hour's work to hew two logs for andirons. The Lazy Man's fire isn't—it needs armloads of kindling to keep it burning.

When the forest is dry, starting a fire is easy. Even these methods work well. As a matter of fact, simply dropping a lighted match on the ground may start a blaze. However, what happens when tinder is damp, fuel is soggy, the wind is blowing, and there's a downpour that will drown a bullhead? The fancy fire structures literally fall apart at the seams. There is only one type of fire to build—one that will burn, no matter what the weather is doing.

Three components go into a campfire: tinder, kindling, and fuel wood. Forget the old saw about using only two matches. Use as many as you need. However, if you have suitable tinder, chances are you'll need only one. Tinder can be almost any highly flammable substance: dry twigs, bark (white birch is best but don't peel live trees!), waste food wrappers, even yesterday's funnies. The "slick" type of magazine paper burns poorly by itself, but newsprint is excellent. Man-made fire starters are a badge of efficiency, not the mark of an amateur. A professional woodsman will use anything that's handy! So don't hesitate to use bits of candles, dabs of "canned heat," or homemade tinders such as twisted bits of newspaper soaked in paraffin. Starting a campfire should be a pleasant chore, not a handicap event.

The Prayer Stick is seldom a necessity among family campers, but no youngster should go camping without learning how to whittle one. It should be whittled from a stick of seasoned, split softwood. The secret to safe and successful whittling lies in bracing the stick vertically against a log or stump with one hand. With the other clasping a sharp knife firmly, whittle thin shavings from the edges of the stick, but don't cut them off completely. The shavings should

Not a campfire necessity, but every youngster should learn to whittle a Prayer Stick in this day of the return to basic fuels. ELEANOR RIVIERE

curl so that they bristle in all directions. Two or three of these, laid one atop the other under a few sticks of kindling, will almost guarantee a fire. Children old enough to use a knife will enjoy a great sense of primitive accomplishment making these, a feeling of attainment denied them by modern family camping.

The use of gasoline, naphtha, or kerosene as fire starters or aids is about as safe as poking a bull moose with a sharp stick. Gasoline should *never* be used. In fact, it is not only dangerous but also inefficient—burning out too quickly. Kerosene may be used with safety only when no flames or glowing coals exist. Pouring kerosene on a bed of hot coals is tantamount to tossing a match into a keg of gunpowder.

As for kindling, dry softwood is best. This comes from evergreen trees. To most family campers, however, all evergreens are "pine trees," and few know one hardwood from another once the leaves have been shed. What's more, the campground woodpile will likely be a mixture of hard and soft species, difficult to identify. One simple method doesn't require a degree in forestry. Gouge the surface of one stick with a thumbnail. If it's hardwood, you'll make little or no headway into the wood fibers. If it's softwood, you'll easily press the edge of the thumbnail into the wood.

Fire-building failures are the result of (1) using wet or damp kindling or (2) attempting to ignite kindling that has not been split finely enough. The first problem can be eliminated by keeping a supply under cover. If the kindling supply is already wet when you arrive, split it. You'll find the interior wood relatively dry. The second problem is overcome by splitting sticks no more than one-half-to-three-quarters-inch thick. After all, you can't expect a tiny flame to ignite a bolt of wood the size of a baseball bat!

Another common source of failure is the heaping of too much wood on the fire before it gets under way healthily—smothering the tinder and cutting off the oxygen without which no fire will burn. To avoid this smothering of infant flames, lay a "base stick," two to three inches in diameter, in the fireplace. Place the tinder, loosely piled, or if paper, crumpled, beside the stick. If Prayer Sticks are used, rest two or three against the base stick. Atop the tinder, place kindling so that it too rests on or over the stick. Light the

Dry kindling is always available inside a "dry stub," which the author is prying open with his ax.
ELEANOR RIVIERE

tinder *as close to the ground as possible* and to *windward,* so that the wind will blow the flame *into* the fuel. The most common mistake in lighting a fire is to apply the match on the lee or downwind side, in an attempt to shield its flame. This results in the flame being blown *away* from the tinder.

As the fire gets under way, the weight of the kindling will settle the burning tinder, but the former *cannot drop below* the level of the base stick. Hence, air can circulate freely *under* the flames, where it's most needed. Always add wood in a crisscross fashion so that flames can work their way upward between sticks. Some methodical campers tend to lay fuel wood neatly parallel and close together, cutting off upward draft.

If you're lucky enough to have a choice, use softwood for quick, hot fires. They'll heat a can of soup or boil up a pot of coffee in little time. For more extensive cooking, use hardwood. Three or four sticks of two-inch-thick maple, for

example, will burn for fifteen to twenty minutes and still provide coals hot enough for another fifteen minutes. Split hardwood burns more readily than unsplit or round billets.

Much has been written about the various types of fireplaces a camper can devise, along with numerous ingenious pot hooks, cranes, and even my favorite dingle stick, but it isn't often that family campers pitch their outfits where cutting of trees or brush is permitted. Most family camping areas provide fireplaces equipped with some sort of steel or iron grille upon which to rest cooking utensils.

Generally a saw is unnecessary on a family-type campground where wood is provided cut-to-length. However, it may occasionally come in handy. Bow-type saws, some of which fold and enclose the blade for protection during transportation, are efficient if the blade is at least 20" to 24" long. Shorter blades are suitable only for cutting sticks that are more easily and quickly cut with one or two strokes of an ax.

I suggest an ax because, frankly, I have a "thing" about hatchets. I'll grant that they are adequate for light work—splitting kindling or cutting thin sticks of fuel wood. But "adequate" is hardly a recommendation.

The hatchet is the world's most inefficient cutting tool and one of the most dangerous. Here's why: The chopping or cutting stroke is made with one arm, thus there is less control over the cutting edge; because of the short handle, you must stand closer to your target (many campers kneel, which is worse), thus increasing the chances of injury; and because the hatchet's light head won't bite readily into wood fibers, there's a greater chance of glancing; finally, the lightweight head requires that it be *driven* into the wood, at the expense of much greater effort by the axman.

By way of contrast, it's easier to lift a three-pound ax with two hands than it is to swing a 1½-pound hatchet with one. Because *two* hands grasp the handle, there's better control and less chance of glancing. The added weight of the ax lends greater momentum to your swing and the edge bites deeply, and since the handle is longer —26 to 28 inches instead of 12 to 16 inches—you can stand safely away from the target area. Whether you merely split wood occasionally or enjoy a full-fledged workout at the campground woodpile, the best tool is the three-pound pole ax. If this seems like too much to handle, compromise and buy a 2½-pound canoe ax or the famed Hudson's Bay ax, both available in 24-inch handle length. Keeping the edge sharp will not only make your work easier but also safer. A sharp-edged ax will bite in where it's aimed. A dull one glances off, sometimes into a shin or ankle.

Whether you decide on an ax or a hatchet, splitting should be done on a chopping block or log, never on bare ground, where missing a stroke might drive the edge into the rocky earth —considered to have a dulling effect on the edge. Standard technique among untrained beginners calls for holding a wood block vertically with one hand while raising the ax with the other. As the ax descends, the lower hand is withdrawn, sometimes with sufficient speed to avoid amputation. Too often, however, timing is off, and the ax strikes before fingers are completely clear. Sometimes, too, the fingers may be withdrawn too soon, so that the stick topples. The ax then strikes a glancing blow, all too often into the chopper's leg.

Good ax technique at the splitting block is simplicity itself. Place the edge of the tool against the upper surface of the wood to be split. Now lift both the wood and ax as one and drop them gently together against the chopping block, with only enough force to drive the ax bit into the wood. You can now place *both* hands on the ax handle and lift it and the wood. This time, drop the two together onto the chopping block with force. This will usually split most straight-grained woods. With some, however, whose grain may be twisted, it will require two or more blows, but at no time will your fingers be in danger. Splitting wood is a rather pleasurable chore if done properly. It should not be hard work, and there's rarely a need for exerting great force. It's not even necessary to grunt. Woodsmen, strangely enough, don't enjoy chopping. This is hard work, but splitting is another matter. I've never known one who didn't relish an occasional half hour at the splitting block.

Our lives are so thoroughly mechanized that there is little need for physical exertion, and thus we cheat ourselves. Nowhere does a man get to know himself better than at the woodpile. And nowhere does he get to understand his fellow man more easily than around a campfire. What's more, campfire smoke is a nice sort of pollution. We should have more of it.

Chapter 8

THE CAMPSTOVE

Only propane and gasoline stoves have attained any degree of acceptance among family campers. While kerosene has the greatest heat potential (132,500 BTUs per gallon),[1] kerosene stoves suitable for cooking family meals at a campground are almost nonexistent. Methyl alcohol's heat values (64,000 BTUs) are too low for efficient large-scale cooking. Alcohol *will* do the job, but it's slow. Butane (101,000 BTUs) is a superb fuel but is generally available in the North only in tiny disposable cans, too small to allow sufficient vaporization in a cool climate. Butane stoves, too, are small—usually one-burner, compact, and lightweight units for use by backpackers and climbers, and generally inadequate for family cooking. There remain, then, only gasoline, propane, and naphtha.

Among tent campers (recreational vehicles are almost invariably equipped with propane appliances) the two-burner gasoline stove, compact, light, efficient, and inexpensive, is popular. Operating cost is low, too, under $.07 per burner per hour. Three-burner gasoline stoves are also available, naturally somewhat heavier and bulkier.

Some, notably the Thermos brand, are designed to burn any type of gasoline, including leaded fuel used in automobiles. Coleman stoves, on the other hand, require white, marine, or unleaded gasoline. But there is an even better fuel that can be used in any gasoline stove, domestic or imported. This is naphtha (121,000 BTUs), now packaged commercially as Coleman fuel. I owe no allegiance to the Coleman Company, but a superb product must be recognized. Using naphtha, or Coleman fuel, in several stoves over many years, I've never had a malfunction due to carbon or clogging. Admittedly, it's more expensive, costing perhaps three times the price of gasoline, but the convenient packaging and efficiency offset the extra cost for many campers. However, if you're on a tight budget, white, marine, or unleaded gasoline will give excellent service in *any* gasoline stove.

Not all campers agree that the gasoline stove is ideal. Many object to the necessary refilling and almost inevitable spilling. Some consider pumping to build and maintain tank pressure to be a nuisance. Women often fear lighting a gasoline stove, having been frightened by a "flareup." Too, considerable cussing has been done at replacing generators or clearing clogged jets. Beginners are frequently baffled by the necessity of manipulating two valves.

In all fairness to gasoline stoves, they are easy and safe to operate once you've acquired the knack. Malfunctions are usually due to human error. I long ago lost track of the stoves that I've tinkered for frustrated campers, but I can recall only one that needed actual repair—an off-beat brand in need of a new generator.

American-made gasoline campstoves are "instant lighting," which means they require no priming or preheating of the generator, as do some European "petrol" stoves. Once the tank has been pumped to proper pressure, the light-

[1] BTU stands for British thermal unit, equivalent to the heat required to raise the temperature of 1 pound of water 1 degree Fahrenheit, starting at or near 39.2 degrees Fahrenheit.

The famed Coleman 2-burner, on a folding stand and equipped with side shelves. COLEMAN

ing procedure differs only slightly among domestic models. First, a starter lever or knob must be turned. This controls the amount of fuel that will feed through the burner. Opening a second valve allows air to enter the fuel wire,

above the level of the fuel in the tank. The two then mix to form a fine spray in the generator before passing on to the burner. Usually a camper applies a lighted match as soon as he has opened the second valve. In many instances gasoline and air have not thoroughly mixed immediately, and only air comes through the burner orifices. This blows out the match. While the camper struggles with a second or third match—it's at such a time that matches break or won't light—gasoline vapors begin to pour through the burner. If the struggle with ornery matches is slightly prolonged, an excess of vapors may accumulate, then condense and fall into the bottom of the stove casing. Finally a match lights and there's an explosive "POOF!"

To avoid this, listen closely to the sound coming from the burner once the second valve is opened. You'll note that at first there may be only a "dry" hiss. This is nothing but air. Don't apply the match yet. In a moment you'll hear the hiss take on a "wet" or sizzling sound, possibly a faint sputtering. This is the sound of gasoline, mixed with air, coming through, and it signals for a lighted match.

It's important that the generator valve (the second to be opened) be opened wide so that an active and hot flame envelops the generator to heat it. The generator is simply a mixing chamber perched over a burner. When heated, this chamber changes the air-gas mixture into

The Thermos 2-burner model, which burns either leaded or unleaded gasoline. THERMOS

a vapor before feeding it through the burner. At first the flame may be yellowish and somewhat high, but this will usually last but a minute or two. When the flame turns blue, shut off the first valve completely. Failure to do this will result in quick loss of pressure in the tank. Once the valve is shut, additional pressure may be added to the tank, to the extent of fifteen to twenty strokes of the pump.

Don't overdo this pumping, however. Excess pressure will cause the flame to lift away from the burner erratically. At high altitudes, where atmospheric pressures may be diminished, it's often best to light the stove with only slight pressure in the tank. Otherwise some raw gasoline may flood the stove and cause the "flareup" I've just described. This needn't be an alarming situation, however. The excess gas will vaporize or burn quite quickly.

Another cause of the flame's lifting away from the burner is a too-lean air-gas mixture, the result of gum or corrosion on the tip of the cleaning needle, which extends down through the vertical fuel line to the bottom of the tank. Clean the needle point carefully—and gently—with fine emery cloth. This usually eliminates this trouble.

Overfilling the tank cuts air space, resulting in a high, yellowish, smoky flame. A studio assistant once filled a new Coleman stove for me minutes before I was due on the air for a TV demonstration of camp cooking. Thousands of viewers then watched me struggle to control a three-foot flame when I lighted the stove! We had to switch from cooking to chatter. It wasn't until after the show was off the air that I discovered the problem, an overfilled tank, full to the brim of the filler spout.

Fill only to the manufacturer's recommendation, usually indicated on the tank. Wipe away any spillage before lighting the stove, or allow it to evaporate. Dirt and burned match heads tend to accumulate in the burner pan, and these will cause yellow, smoky flames that will quickly apply a layer of soot to utensils. Remove the burner cap—a single screw in the center of the burner permits this—and clean away the debris. An old toothbrush is ideal for this chore.

Whenever the stove is to be stored for some time, as during the winter season, flush and drain the tank or allow a small quantity of fuel to burn itself out. This will prevent the accumulation of gum deposits, which may clog the generator and tiny, sensitive jets. After lengthy storage, especially in a warm room, you may find that the pump will not force air into the tank, the plunger sliding freely. This is because the leather washer on the plunger has dried and shrunk. One or two drops of oil on this will cause it to swell almost immediately for a snug fit in the pump cylinder. Too, the gasket in the filler cap may deteriorate with age so that air pressure cannot be maintained in the tank. If this gasket becomes hard and brittle, replace it, a simple task. If you discover this in camp and have no spare, apply a little oil as suggested for the plunger, or soak it overnight in a small quantity of gasoline. If you have occasion to remove the valve assembly from the tank, apply a little bar soap to the threads before screwing the unit back into the tank. This will seal them against leaks.

Probably the only spare part you'll ever need is a generator. Carry a spare, easily installed after removal of the balky one. However, don't tape it to the stove near one of the burners, as a friend did. When he next lit the stove, the heat melted the plastic knob.

The two-burner stove is usually adequate for most camping families. But if you like to unlimber a variety of pots simultaneously for gourmet dining, consider a three-burner model. Or carry one of the tiny single-burner backpackers' stoves as an auxiliary heat source. The Svea is a hiker's favorite, weighing slightly more than one pound, yet capable of boiling a quart of water in about six minutes. Optimus has two models, the larger of which will boil a quart of water in four minutes. It's equipped with a pressure pump, much like Coleman and Thermos stoves. Also marketed by Optimus is a small two-burner model, ideal if space is a problem in your rig.

While the male may invent and improve campstoves, it's the women who come up with clever improvisations for their use. For example, one sprays the inside of the case with Windex, the spray reaching into the corners to loosen accumulated grease and dirt, which then wipes out easily. Another does the same chore with a small paint brush and household ammonia. Some line the interior of the stove with aluminum foil, easily removed, dirt and all. It was a fireman, however, who suggested an excellent and inexpensive fire extinguisher to combat "flareup."

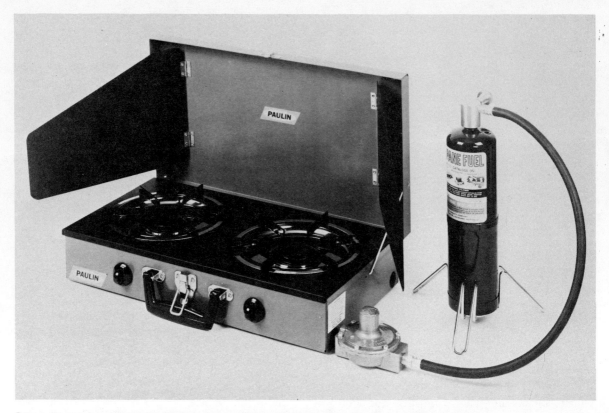

The 2-burner Paulin, operated by a disposable cylinder with pressure regulator. PAULIN

He fills a discarded plastic soap powder bottle with bicarbonate of soda. When flames leap up unduly, he merely points the bottle at the flames and squeezes. The soda kills the flame instantly.

Campers who have used gasoline stoves over the years tend to stick with them, but newcomers are attracted by modern, propane-fired models. Manufacturers recognize this. At least one major producer of gasoline stoves (Coleman) has added a line of propane units.

Propane (92,800 BTUs) appeals strongly to women who may be apprehensive about lighting a gasoline stove, and there are many more such campers than one might suppose. The frequent claims of "no filling, no spilling, no pumping—just turn on the valve and light" bear great weight, and justly so. As an added bonus, propane creates no soot, carbon doesn't clog jets, and the stove itself has fewer than half the number of parts found in a gasoline model. In fact, except for the simple shutoff, there are no parts to wear out.

Propane, also known as "bottle gas," is a liquid petroleum gas piped throughout the coun-

try, where it is then loaded into various-size containers, ranging from 14-ounce disposable cylinders to huge industrial, agricultural, and commercial tanks. It is a liquid that vaporizes without the need for pumping. And it is relatively inexpensive when purchased in bulk tanks that may be refilled. With disposable cylinders, however, you pay more for the container than for the contents! You're buying convenience. Also a disposal problem. Reloading your stove calls simply for removing the empty cylinder and screwing in a new one. Certainly no gasoline stove can be refueled that easily! But what do you do with the steel cylinder? You discard it. It's not biodegradable. It may even explode if tossed into a burning town dump. Worse yet, you'll get no more than 6 hours' burning time from a single cylinder, often less, especially in lanterns. Thus, operating costs run high per hour. As already pointed out, the 14-ounce cylinder is a convenience item. That's all that can be said for it.

Some years ago, propane stove makers introduced a refillable 14-ounce cylinder. Any camper, they proclaimed, could refill it from

A bulk propane tank operating a gasoline stove by means of a converter, actually improving the efficiency of the stove. PAULIN

a larger tank, such as the 20-pounders used on recreational vehicles. The idea fell rather flat. Transferring propane from one container to another by amateur methods is tricky. Also, many campers asked themselves: Why can't I save myself the trouble by using the larger, refillable tank directly?

Campstove makers got the message. Regular 20-pound tanks have a gross weight of about 35 pounds, too heavy for tent campers to juggle, although ideal on recreational vehicles. So they produced smaller bulk tanks that can be refilled with 6, 8, or 10 pounds of gas. Depending upon use, these tanks last from a week to a month; they reduce the cost of gas considerably; and they eliminate a disposal problem.

A growing number of propane dealers, although primarily interested in large bulk sales, have set up refill stations for these little tanks. The gas will cost you somewhat more per pound than its price in a 100-pound residential tank, but it is still far cheaper than that sold in disposable cylinders. Recreational vehicle dealers, too, as well as some campgrounds, have set up

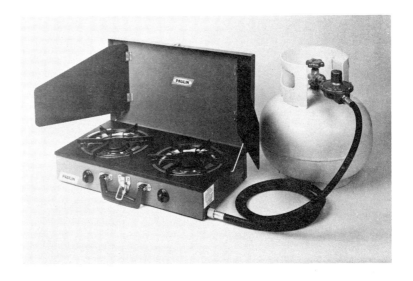

Two-burner stove designed for operation with an economical bulk tank of propane. PAULIN

propane refill stations. At least two directories[2] listing these are available.

Propane's only drawback is the initial cost of equipment, as compared to the price of a gasoline stove. A complete outfit may cost you $40 or more. But remember that you can "turn on the valve and light up," with no filling or spilling, no flareup, no clogged generators.

When you start shopping, you'll run into the terms "high pressure" and "low pressure." Low pressure does not imply poorer efficiency; high pressure does not mean danger. Disposable cylinders are high-pressure types. Bulk tanks, whether 6-pounders, or 100-pound units, use a pressure regulator between the tank and the stove, usually attached directly to the tank. Regulators are used on household installations. These control pressure fed into the burners at "11-inch water column," or 6 ounces. Don't worry about the technicalities.

I've used bulk tank installations at 40 degrees

2 See the Appendix.

below zero and at 94 degrees above zero with no problems. Disposable cylinders, however, are less efficient in cold weather because they are too small to provide for vaporization.

Combining simple precautions and a little knowledge of it as a fuel, propane is as safe as gasoline. Both are, in fact, vaporized liquids as they come through a campstove burner. The difference lies in that propane is "self-pressurized." For example, if the cap on your gasoline can is not closed tightly, only natural evaporation will escape. If the valve on a propane tank is left open, gas will continue to escape until nearly all of it is drained. Being heavier than air, propane tends to gather in low places and, if the correct air-gas combination (this is quite critical) should occur, disaster can accompany the lighting of a match or the dropping of a cigarette spark. Making sure that all hose connections are tight and that valves are turned off snugly when not in use will eliminate this danger.

Chapter 9

LANTERNS AND HEATERS

LANTERNS

One of the most craven defilers of campfire rapture is the camper who lights his two-mantle gasoline lantern as soon as his neighbors have settled themselves about their evening campfires. He not only saturates his own site with an overdose of candlepower, but he illuminates all of those around him with a blinding glare, too! Such senseless brilliance has no place in a campground. The single-mantle lantern casts ample light for camping purposes, breaks fewer mantles, burns less fuel, and certainly annoys fewer neighbors.

We Americans have been conditioned to believe that life in camp without a powerful lantern is impossible. For doing late dishes, reading, tucking the kids in, or for assembling a late-evening snack, light is a necessity, of course. On the other hand, campfire light or the glow of moonlight is soothing to jangled nerves.

It's equally obnoxious for a camper to carry a powerful light on the nightly prebedtime treks to the campground washhouse. This needlessly gives everyone along his route an annoying exposure to temporary blindness.

In my own family we have relied mostly on individual flashlights for most nighttime chores. For walking along campground paths at night, we found that flashlights that cast a wide cone of light are preferable to spotlights that illuminate only a small circular area, often overlooking a tree root, stump, or rock waiting to trip a camper along the dark fringes of the trail. Another advantage of individual flashlights is that others need not be deprived of the use of the lantern whenever one member of the family needs to illuminate a wooded pathway. Our lantern, a one-mantle type, stays hung up in camp, although it may not be used for several evenings in a row.

The gasoline lantern is remarkably efficient and reliable. Occasional repairs or adjustments are usually simple if done by daylight. Therefore, if you're going to need your lantern, light it before complete darkness has fallen. If the lantern decides to balk and needs tinkering, you can see what you are doing. Routine care of a lantern includes the occasional cleaning of the globe and shade, which tend to accumulate soot. Old-time users of kerosene lamps found that newspaper applied to the inside surfaces resulted in a high gloss that cast a bright light. This is still true, although paper towels, napkins, or facial tissues serve well. Before leaving on a camping trip, check the washer in the filler cap, which serves as a seal to make the tank airtight. If dried or brittle, a drop of oil will usually cause it to swell and fit snugly. If this fails, it's a simple matter to replace it. Pressure in the tank can be tested by applying soap bubbles around the cap. If a leak exists, you'll hear a faint hiss or see the tiny bubbles grow and burst. It's wise occasionally to oil the leather washer in the pump plunger since, if this has dried out, you'll find it impossible to build up pressure.

With the advent of propane stoves for camping have come bottled-gas lanterns, some operating from disposable cans or cylinders, others

Gasoline lantern with reflector and handle. COLEMAN

Convenient, efficient, and highly portable, the "direct cylinder" propane light may prove costly to operate. PAULIN

jointly with a stove from a single bulk tank. Light from these lanterns is comparable to that cast by a single-mantle gasoline lantern or a 50-watt electric bulb. The type that uses disposable cans or cylinders has the flexibility of the gasoline lantern, since fuel is self-contained. Those operating from a bulk tank, however, will bring up short any camper who tries to walk with the lantern, usually at the end of a 6-to-12-foot hose. If propane is used for cooking, bottled-gas lanterns are highly practical, since you will then be carrying only one fuel.

When it comes to using disposable cylinders, however, the same is true of lanterns as of stoves. Fuel costs rise sharply.

Some years ago I fell heir to several cases of 14-ounce disposable propane cylinders. Their use on tenting trips is more of a hindrance than a help, so I hauled them to my remote cabin in the Maine woods where, before we acquired Aladdin lamps, we used propane camp lanterns. We spent almost seven months in the cabin that year. I've no idea how many cylinders we consumed, but I do remember that none lasted more than six to seven hours. Some petered out sooner. With darkness coming early in the fall, each long evening exhausted a cylinder. Had we purchased them at retail our daily lighting cost would have soared to more than one dollar. Granted, the light was excellent for reading (no TV in our cabin!), and certainly the lights were convenient to reload and light. But for prolonged use, I consider the cost prohibitive. Used an hour or two following a long summer twilight in a campground, they are acceptable.

If you favor a campstove operating from a bulk propane tank, look into the several lanterns that may be attached to the same tank. Your gas consumption will increase, of course, but the per-hour cost is far below that of cylinders. You can't move such a lantern more than six to twelve feet (the length of standard hoses), but it does provide an ample, soft light.

Propane lanterns are far less temperamental than gasoline lights and, too, like the stoves, they're easier to light. The most trouble you're likely to encounter will consist of changing a mantle. These are very similar to those used on gasoline lanterns. In fact, they are interchangeable.

If you hang a lighted gasoline or propane lantern by its bail for more than a few minutes,

don't grasp the latter with a bare hand or you'll
acquire a nasty burn. The bail gets hot. Obviously, too, avoid hanging a lighted lantern
close to a canvas wall or tent roof. Toting gasoline or propane lanterns in the jumble of equipment in a typical camper's car presents problems. After breaking several globes and enough
mantles to illuminate Yellowstone National Park,
I finally built plywood lantern boxes—these
lined with foam rubber to cushion the lanterns.
We still break occasional mantles, but it's been
years since we've had to replace a globe. Carrying cases are now available from some lantern
manufacturers, designed to fit their lanterns, of
course.

Like their campstove counterparts, kerosene
lanterns are not popular. The old-fashioned
Dietz light—the one you see on TV being thrown
into a hay mow to start a barn fire—is fully adequate for most camping purposes, but it's a rare
sight in today's campgrounds. More sophisticated
kerosene lanterns of European origin—the Optimus, for example—are of superb workmanship
and cast light comparable to that of a 200-watt
bulb, at low cost. I have an Optimus but keep
it at the cabin.

More readily accepted by campers are battery-
operated electric lanterns. These offer the port-
ability of the gasoline type, yet eliminate the
need for frequent change of cylinders or refuel-
ing with flammable liquids. Bulbs must be replaced occasionally, of course. Batteries wear
out, too, but with intermittent use, some will last
a complete season. Fluorescent models give off a
soft light, some of these rechargeable from a
household 110-volt outlet or a car's 12-volt system, each charge good for about 20 hours. A
rheostat controls light output.

One of my favorite camp lights is the little
Mallory, weighing barely 4 ounces and less than
4 inches long and operated by a pair of No. AA
batteries. The manufacturer claims a 200-foot
beam, but I seldom have need for such farsight-
edness in the darkness. I keep it in my back
pocket for little chores about the campsite.

Battery lights lack the brilliance of the larger
gasoline lanterns, but they have advantages. For
example, they're safe to use even in a snugly
enclosed area, and a quick flick of the switch
brings instant light. There's no need to grope for
a match. Powerful spotlights that "shine a mile"
are poor choices, however, being better suited

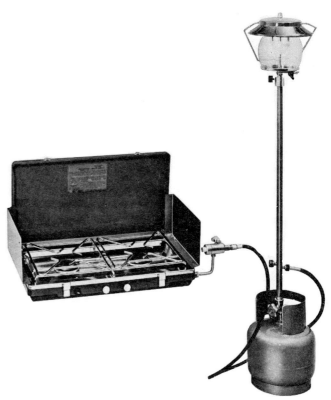

*Economical cooking and lighting from a bulk tank
that supplies both units.* TRAILBLAZER/WINCHESTER

Carrying case protects lantern against breakage.
COLEMAN

Fluorescent rechargeable light is somewhat heavy but gives off a soft light, more than adequate for camping. COLEMAN

Smaller fluorescent type of rechargeable lantern. NIGHTWIN

to night boating than to camping. Their mighty beams are annoying to neighbors and hardly necessary to search out the depths of a duffel bag. The flood lamp is more practical, if less spectacular. A feature we've found useful on at least two occasions when tires had to be changed alongside a dark road is the built-in red flashing, blinking bulb, which warns oncoming traffic of roadside trouble.

It may be carrying camp lighting to extremes, but we have friends who "wire" their campsites with 2 12-volt bulbs, one in their tent, another over the picnic table—these powered by means of spring clips attached directly to the car's battery. One bulb will operate about 6 hours without noticeable drain on the battery; 2 bulbs, of course, will reduce this margin to about 3 hours. Longer periods of use require that the car's engine be run 15 to 20 minutes to recharge the battery.

All in all, illuminating a campsite today is a far cry from the days when we inserted a candle through a hole punctured in the side of an empty spaghetti-and-meatball can.

HEATERS

Except for folding camping trailers, recreational vehicles are usually equipped with vented propane heaters meeting specified safety standards. Folding trailers, however, are frequently sold without heating appliances, especially the so-called "economy" models. And, of course, tents lack such built-in luxury. Portable heaters come into use.

All burners consume oxygen, some more than others, and while most tents suffer sufficiently from gaps to replenish this oxygen, the replacement may not be adequate to prevent illness. It's doubtful that asphyxiation can occur in a canvas shelter, but it's not unusual for occupants to suffer from nausea or headaches following a rainy night in a heated tent. This is due to the fact that moisture tightens fabric weave, cutting down the normal passage of air through it. Leaving a door or window partially open admits fresh air, of course, but it also permits the escape of heat. Nevertheless, some degree of ventilation may be necessary in a well-closed tent or folding camper.

Carbon monoxide, insidiously deadly since it

is odorless, can and does result from the burning of virtually any fuel. Catalytic heaters come close to perfect combustion of fuel, and early advertising of these occasionally boasted "no carbon monoxide." Such claims are notably absent tóday. I'm not condemning tent heaters, but nonetheless the best and safest source of all-night warmth is a good sleeping bag!

For years I've campaigned against all-night heating of camping shelters, even if the temperature drops to well below freezing. I'm not insisting that campers suffer spartan discomforts though. As long as someone remains awake, by all means enjoy the comfort of a heated shelter. For evening lounging, for a cool or rainy day, or for climbing into a nightshirt prior to retiring when there's frost in the air, there's need for a heater. However, just before climbing into my sleeping bag, I shut mine off—tightly. In the morning, if the sun has failed to warm the tent, I can reach over without leaving the warmth of my bunk to relight the heater. While I'm waiting for atmospheric conditions conducive to the graceful donning of britches, I contemplate the wonders of modern conveniences in camping. This doesn't take long.

Newcomers to camping are often surprised that a canvas shelter can be heated at all. After all, the walls *are* thin and porous. As a matter of fact, canvas detains heat rather well. I use the word "detain" because this is exactly what occurs. As soon as the heat source is eliminated, a tent will cool to outside temperature in a matter of minutes.

A lantern may suffice to heat a small tent, even at freezing temperatures, but larger shelters and folding trailers need a full-fledged heater. With regard to improvised heating, under no circumstances bring glowing charcoal into any sort of camper or closed tent. Even after the glow has died, hot charcoal continues to produce deadly fumes. At high altitudes, where combustion may not be complete, the danger is even greater.

I have occasionally used a small propane or butane campstove to heat one of my small tents, but only to dispel a morning chill, never for all-night comfort.

Wood-burning stoves remain on the camping scene, but since few family-type tents are equipped with suitable "smoke hole" outlets, these stoves are used primarily by guides, outfitters,

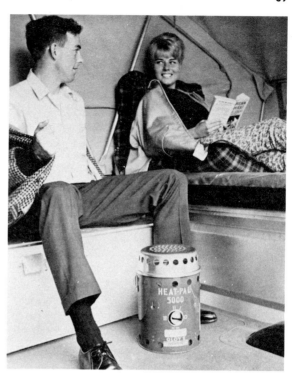

Alcohol-burning portable tent and camper heater.
GLOY IMPORTS

and hunters. They are remarkably efficient and safe if placed sufficiently far from canvas walls and roof. And it takes only a surprisingly small fire to heat most tents, up to 10′×14′. But such stoves are generally bulky or heavy, even the collapsible models. However, if such heaters appeal to you, look into the various models— Sims, Sheepherder, Raemco. Most large camping equipment outfitters list them in their catalogs.

When family camping showed signs of mushrooming, during the late fifties and early sixties, alcohol-burning space heaters were common, some of them little more than fancied-up five-gallon cans with a wick and a burner. These were economical, fairly efficient, and safe, but "slow to fire up." Currently, the Gloy "Heat Pal" seems to be the sole survivor among alcohol heaters. Imported from Sweden, the heater has a large wick, which holds the fuel in suspension for combustion and is capable of up to 5,000 BTUs. It can also be converted to a one-burner cookstove. The fuel is denatured or solvent alcohol available at most hardware or paint stores.

Other fuels that are used in portable camp-

Infrared propane heater beams heat directionally.
PAULIN

Infrared heater head operating from bulk tank.
PAULIN

ing heaters include butane, propane, white gasoline, and naphtha or Coleman fuel.

Butane heaters are tiny units, operating from 6½-ounce cans and producing up to 2,500 BTUs. They're efficient but obviously limited to use in small tents, such as a backpacker's shelter. In a family-size tent, you'll need two to three times that BTU output.

Heaters in this category are of the radiant and/or catalytic type. Radiant heaters are sometimes referred to as "infrared" heaters, operating from either disposable cylinders or bulk propane tanks. This type of unit "aims" its warmth, shooting it away from a reflector much like a spotlight sends out a light beam. Heat can be concentrated in one area, although as it accumulates in a shelter such units then actually become space heaters. I hesitate to venture into the medical world, but infrared rays are supposed to penetrate body tissues with beneficial therapeutic effect. Their heat is like that of the sun, and they seemingly put out more BTUs than their fuel ratings might indicate. This doesn't mean that an infrared radiant heater might be used as a sunlamp. You can't get a suntan from its heat since it does not produce any ultraviolet rays. Infrared rays are strictly heat rays.

Infrared rays are produced from gas by burning the latter in ceramic units, in double-metal mantles or within dual metal screens. Replacing these burner units becomes necessary in time, but generally they will last some 500 hours or more and are easily replaced at small cost.

One of the principal makers of such heaters is Paulin,[1] whose units are rated at 8,000 BTUs, operating from disposable cylinders or bulk tanks. Other firms make similar heaters, but what makes Paulin different is its refreshing and straightforwardly honest assessment of its heaters. In bold-face type (not the usual fine print), Paulin states clearly: **"Heater will operate 3 hours on 14-ounce cylinder."** This from a firm that sells disposable cylinders! Even I can figure out that operating costs may run comparatively high. In smaller, though still bold-face type, Paulin's specifications add: **"Heater operates 70 to 100 hours on 20-lb. tank."** At this point, if I were a would-be purchaser of a tent heater, I'd take a second look at Paulin. Such honesty lends credence to advertising claims re-

[1] See the Appendix.

Bulk-tank infrared heater head tilted to serve as cookstove. PAULIN

garding its combination heater and cooker adapted to bulk-tank use with an optional safety valve that turns off the gas supply should the flame be extinguished. And its claim of operating costs of less than $.03 per hour from a bulk tank is realistic.

Other firms offer this type of heater, including the Winchester/Trailblazer model, which turns out up to 5,000 BTUs but operates only on disposable cylinders. Such heaters are at maximum output within fifteen seconds of lighting.

Catalytic heaters, though popular, are a mystery to most campers. And, frankly, I'm a little fuzzy about them, too! There is no open flame; few if any moving parts; paper or clothing brushing the heater will not ignite; nor will catastrophe result if the heater is accidentally kicked over. Yet such heaters produce up to 10,000 BTUs.

Most manufacturers of catalytic heaters apparently don't want to clutter a would-be buyer's mind with specifics, so they offer only generalities and vague, though glowing, descriptions. One exception is Zebco Division of Brunswick Corporation.[2] Its catalog clearly and concisely explains the principle of catalytic combustion with a commendable absence of advertising gobbledygook—and I quote:

[2] See the Appendix.

The catalytic principle on which Traveler (Zebco) heaters operate involves the flameless oxidation of propane vapor in the presence of a platinum catalyst. The heating pad of the unit is composed of a ceramic fibrous material which is highly heat-reflective. This pad is impregnated with a catalyst composed of platinum and other rare earth metals. When combustion occurs on the face of the heating pad, the presence of the platinum catalyst causes the propane vapor to ignite and oxidize at a much lower temperature than is necessary to produce flames. (In flame-producing combustion, propane ignites at approximately 1,100° F and combustion is sustained at 1,300° to 1,400° F. In catalytic combustion, ignition occurs at approximately 275° F and combustion is sustained at 700° to 800° F.) The heat produced by catalytic combustion is radiant, infra-red heat. Radiant heat, like light waves, travels in a straight line and is absorbed by the solid objects it strikes. This means that more of the Traveler's heat reaches you, and less is dissipated by the surrounding air. And radiant heat is not affected by atmospheric conditions, such as wind, altitude changes, etc. The life of the catalyst pad is unlimited, since neither the pad nor the platinum catalyst is consumed or altered in any way by the combustion process.

Don't be misled by the relatively low combustion temperatures quoted above. These do not

Catalytic propane heater, among the safest of all heaters, with BTU output of up to 10,000. ZEBCO

side down for a few moments until a small amount of fuel appears on the heating pad. The heater is then righted and lighted. The initial flame will burn down quickly, but it may be fifteen to twenty minutes before full heat output is felt.

The process is actually a simple one, and this type of heater may be a better choice if your campstove and lantern are fired by white gas or Coleman fuel.

Modern portable heaters for camping are as safe as technology can make them. Malfunctions are rare, but there is good reason for every manufacturer's warning that the heaters be used only in a ventilated area, never in a tightly closed camper or tent. Even then I refuse to sleep with any of them. To dispel evening chill, rainy-day dampness, or early morning frost, they're superb appliances; but for nighttime comfort I turn off the heater and climb into a sleeping bag.

indicate low heat-output. On the contrary, catalytic heaters are capable of 4,000 to 10,000 BTUs.

Zebco has several models within this range, one of which converts into a cookstove simply by tilting the burner face into a horizontal position. Winchester's Trailblazer brand produces up to 7,000 BTUs and includes a pilot light, plus a spark-type instant igniter, eliminating the need for matches. A Primus model beams heat in two directions at a 12,000-BTU level. Coleman's heaters are capable of variable output, from 4,000 to 10,000 BTUs.

All may be operated on disposable cylinders or bulk tanks, except the Winchester/Trailblazer, which is designed for use with disposable cylinders, with provisions for housing three of these in the heater case.

Another style of catalytic heater is drum-shaped and fired by white gasoline or Coleman fuel. Heat output ranges up to 8,000 BTUs. The catalytic principle is much the same as that of heaters burning propane, except that a wick conducts fuel vapors to the heating pad. Once operational, these heaters are as safe as the propane type. However, they should be lighted out of doors. Lighting calls for tipping the heater up-

This propane catalytic heater can be lighted without use of a match. TRAILBLAZER/WINCHESTER

Propane catalytic heater which beams heat in 2 directions, speeding the heating of a camper or tent.
PRIMUS

Variable output catalytic heater can produce heat from 4,000 to 10,000 BTUs. COLEMAN

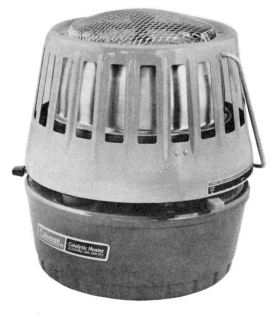

Catalytic heater fired by white gasoline, naphtha, or Coleman fuel, and capable of up to 5,000 BTUs.
COLEMAN

Chapter 10

REFRIGERATION

Since camping is supposed to be a throwback to primitive living, it's not surprising that some of the early devices for refrigeration should persist, at least in camping literature. Still frequently suggested are various dug pits, possibly lined with rocks and covered with boughs, but these were never as efficient as they were portrayed. What's more, digging a pit in a federal or state park is forbidden. Placing a weighted container, such as a wooden box or large can, in a stream or spring is still recommended by some and is practical to some degree. Food placed in the container gets the benefit of cooling from the cold water, but protecting it from prowling raccoons or mink is another matter. I've used such rigs for butter, salt pork, and bacon with success, but for highly perishable foods such as milk, certain meats, and vegetables, refrigeration efficiency is marginal. Another repeatedly suggested "refrigerator" is a wooden box hung in a tree, draped with burlap, which is kept wet by a slowly dripping can of water. Evaporation has a cooling effect, as users of desert water bags know, but it hardly compares to the efficiency of a modern camp ice chest.

Refrigeration experts generally agree that a horizontal box or chest is a better refrigerator than an upright unit with a vertical door. To prove this, stand close to the open door of your household refrigerator. You'll feel the cold air sliding out and striking your legs. Vertical boxes are more convenient, I'll grant. You won't have to burrow under bacon, eggs, and pop bottles to find the hamburger. Too, the ice compartment is generally in the upper half of the box, so that water from the melting ice drips into a tray instead of soaking foods at the bottom of the unit, a failing of the chest. One such camp refrigerator even has a spigot on the ice-water tray. Nevertheless, every time the door is open, most of the cold air slips out, and the melting of ice is accelerated. Further proof lies in the open-top display freezers and refrigerators used in supermarkets. There's no doubt but that chest-type camp refrigerators are more efficient.

Camp ice chests operate more efficiently with block ice than with ice cubes (sometimes sold to campers in plastic bags) simply because the large piece melts more slowly. Two such chests —one permanently stationed at my cabin, the other for car-camping trips—hold a 25-pound block of ice for four to five days, although if the top is not protected from direct sunlight, melting is rapid.

Precooling the chest slows melting. This can be done in a large household freezer or in a grocer's walk-in refrigerator. It will help, too, if you pack as large a proportion of ice to food as possible. Include frozen foods for use early in the trip. Some campers add a layer of "dry ice," since this slows the melting of natural ice. Unfortunately, dry ice is not commonly available. And it should be handled with care, being cold enough to "burn" bare hands. Once arrived at camp, keep the chest in the shade. While preparing meals, make all of the withdrawals at one time, if possible, to avoid repeated openings of the lid. Especially make sure that children close the cover and latch it.

One shortcoming of the chest is that, unless the drain spout is kept open, ice water accumulates in the food compartment so that quite often you may find butter and bacon afloat. Place foods that can be harmed by water so that they can't slip into it. Some of the newer chests have a plastic drain cock on the side. In loading and unloading, care should be used that this isn't broken off. Older-type chests had a recessed drain plug in the bottom, a far more practical arrangement than the "improvement."

Chests are available in a wide range of shapes and sizes, including a shallow model, which slips into the limited space under the folded top of a tent trailer, or into the trunk of compact cars. Linings are usually ABS plastic, frequently ridged for reinforcement. Exterior shells may be plastic or steel with baked-on enamel. The latter is tougher, of course, but my two plastic chests have so far withstood five years of rough use. Insulation, in the better chests, is polyurethane, by far the best.

Simple chests of plastic foam, without lining or outer casing but fitted with a snug-fitting cover, are remarkably efficient and quite inexpensive. Lacking a protective outside casing, they are relatively fragile, however. A raccoon can chew into one in a matter of minutes. Given reasonable care and protection from prowling critters, they're adequate for a family on an equipment budget.

Some types of ice chests can be converted to a freezer/refrigerator combination by inserting a special dry ice unit, which will keep the

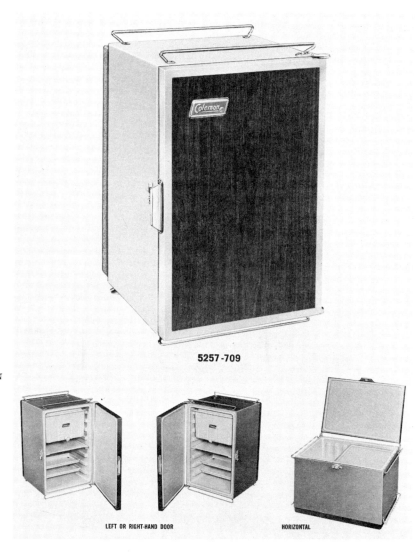

Vertical ice chest is convenient as household refrigerator, and can be used as a horizontal chest. COLEMAN

5257-709

LEFT OR RIGHT-HAND DOOR   HORIZONTAL

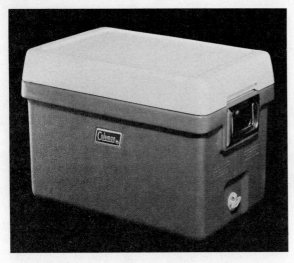

*The author uses two such chests. They're efficient,
but keep them out of direct sunlight.* COLEMAN

freezer portion below zero for some time, plus
making ice cubes in less than an hour. This
unit[1] was designed primarily for ice chests used
in camping trailers.

Miniaturized gas/electric refrigerators have
been praised for years in camping literature, often by writers who never actually used the units

[1] BMC Kardel Freezer insert. See the Appendix.

they described. I have never seen one in use on
a campground but have tested two of them. One
managed to produce a thin shell of ice in the
cube tray; the other failed to function altogether.
These were camping refrigerators selling for
about $100, equal to the price of a half ton of
ice in 25-pound blocks, enough to refrigerate my
camp grub for ten years! Not only did I run
into malfunctions, but the storage capacity in
each of these test boxes was barely 1 cubic
foot. A 6-pack of soft drinks, a slab of bacon,
and a pound of margarine filled them. Like a
cure for the common cold, an efficient and reasonably priced gas/electric camping refrigerator
is a worthwhile objective, but the two that I
tested fell far short.

It would be unfair to condemn all such refrigerators on the strength of the failures of the
two I tested. Paulin, maker of campstoves and
lanterns, markets one that operates on a car's
12-volt system, 110-volt service outlet, or on
propane—up to 40 hours on a 14-ounce cylinder.
It can also be adapted to a bulk tank. Cooling
is by means of an ammonia-hydrogen system. Its
capacity is 1.3 cubic feet, this equal to a space
roughly $12'' \times 12'' \times 16''$, about one third larger
than the units that I tested. These are catalog

*Designed primarily for use in camping trailer ice chests, this unit uses dry ice for a
conversion to a freezer.* KARDEL

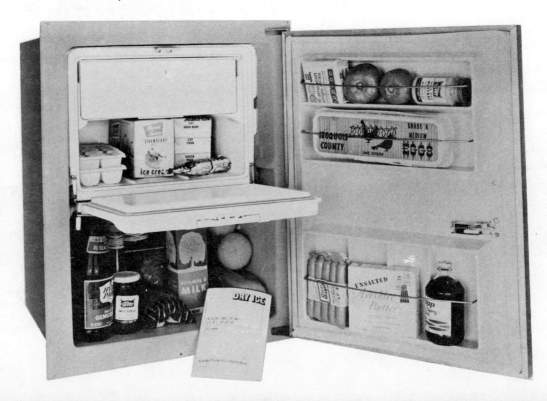

Versatile camp refrigerator operating on gas, 12-V, or 110-V electricity. PAULIN

specifications, and since I have never used one, I suggest it only in the event that you may want to explore mechanical camping refrigeration.

COOLER JUGS

The variety of these is almost overwhelming, ranging from 1 to 3 gallons in capacity, with construction features much like those of campers' ice chests—ABS plastic or polyethylene liners, urethane foam insulation, and plastic or steel casings. Some sort of pouring spout, usually push-button, is standard. Caps or covers are often wide-mouthed and may include several plastic drinking cups. For bulk liquids, such as lemonade, iced tea, or coffee, or any of the myriad fruit-flavored instant mixes, these jugs are ideal. But keep in mind that they are for cold drinks. Rarely can they be used with hot liquids such as soups or coffee. Pouring boiling hot liquid into them may damage the interior plastic liner. For this purpose, use a Thermos-type bottle or cooler —a wide-necked model for soups.

An ice-cube bucket adapts nicely for day-trip lunches. Insulated much like a cooler but with a full-width cover, such a bucket is not necessarily limited to liquids or ice cubes. I attribute this discovery to my wife, Eleanor. She empties an ice cube tray from our kitchen refrigerator into the bucket. Atop the cubes, she places two or three cans of soft drinks, over which go sandwiches wrapped in foil, and our favorite dill pickles encased in plastic wrap. She then seals the cover with masking tape. There was never a more compact, better-refrigerated lunch for a summertime day trip!

Another cooler we use has a galvanized-iron exterior, lacking glamor certainly, but virtually indestructible—the type seen strapped to the side of utility company trucks for quenching the thirst of pole-climbing crews. We acquired our 2-gallon version in 1960 when its urethane foam insulation was relatively new. Our tests, at that time, revealed that a bag of ice cubes would last five days. Now in its fourteenth year of service, the cooler is as good as new. I wouldn't part with it for a farm Down East!

Chapter 11

CAMP KITCHENS

I can't understand why the divorce rate among campers isn't greater. I've seen women sitting on a stump, mixing bowl in their laps, a left foot propping up a fry pan over the fire while hot fat spatters an ankle and pancake batter runs down into her moccasins. Canned goods drop through soggy cardboard cartons, knapsack contents are gooey with maple syrup, and egg whites drip into spaghetti, while Beef Stroganoff evolves as Mrs. Murphy chowder, complete with overalls! Unless it's organized, camp cooking is automatically a handicap event. Divorce, however, is not necessary. A portable camp kitchen can save many a marriage, at the same time making camp cooking relatively easy.

These provide orderly storage and accessibility of ingredients, utensils, tableware, plus a work surface that somewhat approximates a back-home "sideboard." Such units range from knocked-down, assemble-it-yourself units up to deluxe combinations of kitchen, table, chairs, cookstove, and refrigerator requiring a fairly sizable investment.

Outstanding among these is the "Trailcooker,"[1] which closes into a suitcaselike unit, yet when opened includes a 2-burner propane stove, dishes, flatware, a sink, water supply, pots and pans, and work shelf, plus space for a limited amount of nonperishable foods and ingredients. Don't assume that this rig is a *House Beautiful* kitchen, but it is perhaps the most deluxe and convenient commercially offered portable camp kitchen.

Not all family campers can invest heavily in

[1] IHA, Inc. See the Appendix.

camp-cooking convenience. Also, many like to "individualize" their camp kitchens. As a result, many build their own. The "camp box visit" has become the socially accepted practice on campgrounds—object: inspecting other campers' chuck boxes for new ideas. No two camp cooks agree on interior arrangements, size, or contents; hence some clever variations have evolved.

When Eleanor designed, and I built, our first box in 1959, portable camp kitchens were still a novelty, and we produced what we thought were practical and novel innovations. We've looked over dozens—if not hundreds—of boxes since that time. Repeatedly, too, we've asked: "Why didn't *we* think of that?" Practically every kitchen aid not requiring power has been incorporated into chuck boxes.

We included a spillproof 3-compartment drawer to keep camp silver (it's really stainless steel!) sorted. Today, campers often use inexpensive plastic trays for this purpose. Two kitchen knives are stored in leather sheaths bolted to the quarter-inch plywood walls to prevent dulling the edges and to eliminate the chance of cutting a finger. Since we prefer coffee from old-fashioned mugs, we built in a 6-compartment tray, also spillproof, to hold these. During the six years we've used this kitchen, we've never lost a mug through breakage.

Six individual compartments of varying sizes were incorporated into the box, these to keep the contents sorted according to use-frequency for easy finding during meal preparation. The drop door, which serves as a work surface when the box is open, also serves to hold these contents in their respective compartments. There's little or no danger that the catsup will stir itself into the sugar and then spread over the cupcakes.

A tall, narrow compartment is for awkward-to-store items such as long-handled spoons, fork, spatula, aluminum foil, egg beater, and, with a little painstaking fitting, there's even room for a frying pan. A larger compartment was planned to hold bulky cereal and cracker boxes, along with a roll of paper towels. A small cubbyhole restrains easily mislaid items like canned tuna, bouillon cubes, Vienna sausage, seasonings, toothpicks, and matches, yet it will accept a one-pound coffee can nicely. Another tiny storage area is for extra lantern mantles, stove generator, fly dope, and the first-aid kit, the latter kept in the kitchen because most camping injuries are minor cuts and burns that accompany meal preparations. Still another compartment is a "catch-all" for large cans, while another section holds—with little room to spare, I'll grant—a cook kit, dining plates, muffin tin, and whatever else we can manage to cram into it. We also built in a small metal breadbox that we found, after a long search, in a Minnesota country hardware store. This is removable for cleaning. We find, too, that by removing freeze-dried foods from their cartons, we can jam several aluminum envelopes in among cans and other containers.

Through the years we've copied other ideas we've liked in other campers' portable kitchens. For example, we attached a wall-type can opener, which can be removed from its permanently attached bracket for storage inside during travel. With two teen-agers in the family, a bottle-cap remover became necessary. This is bolted to the outside of the cabinet. Then we added a paper-towel dispenser and pegboard hangers for dish mop and towels. We drew the line, however, at attaching a fluorescent light, which could have been powered from the car's cigarette lighter, although we've seen a number of boxes rigged in this manner for late-evening coffee klatches. We've seen several boxes that held small card-file drawers for recipes, and we've noted a great variety of compact canister sets, some of them coffee cans painted and labeled. Plastic dishpans are often included.

The careful and leisurely building of a portable camp kitchen can be a fine wintertime project, in preparation for summer camping—particularly for a camper who is adept with tools and has a home workshop. For the camper who has neither special skills nor tools, an adult-education class in woodworking at a local high school offers not only professional help but access to fine power tools. It's best to work from a set of plans.

The plan included in this chapter may suit you perfectly, but don't hesitate to alter it if some variation will better fit your needs. The

Superdeluxe portable camp kitchen is the ultimate in convenience at mealtime. TRAILCOOKER

*The author's homemade camp
kitchen has a fold-down cover for
a work surface.* RIVIERE

secret to a successful portable camp kitchen is to buy or build one that will be convenient for *you*.

There is no reason, of course, why you can't use a "home drawn" layout. Eleanor and I roughed out our plans by assembling utensils and food packages to be included in our box. On the living room floor we sorted these according to size and frequency of use. Compartments were then laid out on large sheets of white wrapping paper to fit each assortment. Full-size drawings are generally easier to make than scale sketches.

Most commercially built camp kitchens are of half-inch plywood and are excessively heavy even before being filled. In building several of these over the years, I've found that quarter-inch plywood is adequate for the box itself, while the drop door, which converts to a work shelf, is best made of half-inch stock for sturdiness. However, since it is difficult to butt edges of quarter-inch stock (it won't accept wood screws and has too narrow a surface for gluing), corner battens were used for assembly.

*A compartmented tray protects
coffee mugs against breakage.*
RIVIERE

Even a breadbox. RIVIERE

For economy, you can use "good-one-side," interior-type plywood known as "A-D" grade. This has minor defects on one side only, but these can be hidden by facing them into the box. All surfaces, particularly the exposed edges, should be given a double coat of enamel or varnish to keep out moisture. Otherwise, the plywood layers may ripple if they get wet. However, at very slight additional cost, waterproof marine-grade plywood will guarantee against this. The working surface of the drop door may be covered with Masonite or Formica for an easy-to-clean and attractive finish.

Rope handles are less expensive than metal, and they won't interfere with packing the kitchen into tight places. U-shaped metal drawer pulls, either solid or folding, may be used and, frankly, these are more gentle on the hands when you're toting a heavily laden box.

Removable legs of 1"×3" hardwood stock may be attached to the boxes by bolting them to the sides by means of small bolts and wing nuts. The latter will help speed removal. Some set their camp kitchens on folding campstove stands, but we've found most of these rather unsteady.

A close relative of the portable camp kitchen is the chuck box, essentially a simple chest, although the name is often—erroneously—applied to a camp kitchen. Early chuck boxes were a variation of the pannier carried by western pack horses. Another early design was devised by canoemen who built their boxes to fit the rounded contour of a canoe bottom. These often included shoulder straps for toting over portages.

I assembled mine of quarter-inch plywood some fourteen years ago—14" wide, 12" deep, and 30" long—with rope handles, well coated with paint to protect it against moisture, and held together with brass screws. It has been horrendously abused over the years, on portages, in canoes, in the rear deck of various Jeeps and Scouts, from Georgia to Quebec, from Maine to British Columbia. Although planned for toting the grub supply, it has proved a beautifully convenient catch-all, far more convenient than any duffel bag, pack basket, or knapsack.

My chuck box serves as a memory bank. If I remember to take the box along, I'll forget no essentials. Permanently stored in it are freeze-dried foods (enough for a couple of days), a can opener (you can open a can with an ax, but it's not a socially acceptable procedure), odds and ends of cooking gear (tea pail and a

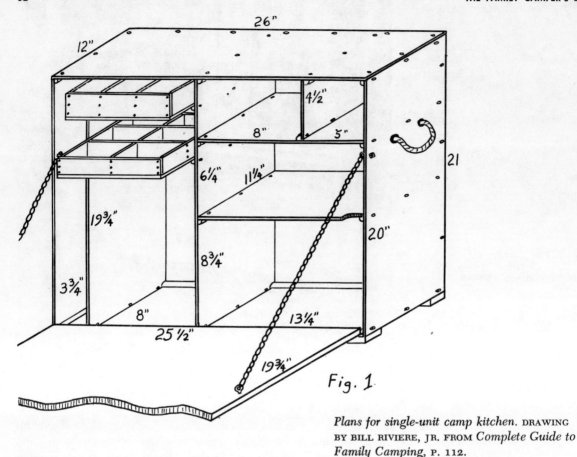

Plans for single-unit camp kitchen. DRAWING BY BILL RIVIERE, JR. FROM *Complete Guide to Family Camping,* P. 112.

six-inch skillet); waterproofed matches, a small butane stove, first-aid kit, one candle stub, and a 50-foot length of nylon cord. These items are the box's permanent residents. When going on a trip, I add additional grub and cooking utensils, according to the duration and type of trip.

While chuck boxes and portable camp kitchens can hardly be classified as absolute necessities, they do eliminate much of the chaos that may accompany meal preparation in camp. They represent, and offer, orderliness. Husbands of reluctant wives take note: Chuck boxes and camp kitchens have enticed many a demurring woman into the wilds.

Easy-to-build chuck box stores cooking gear and grub. WENZEL

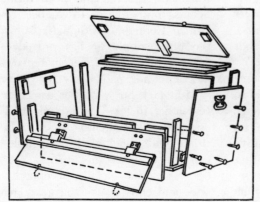

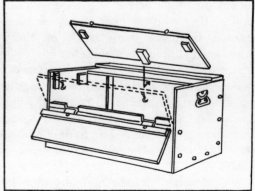

Chapter 12

POTHOOKS AND PANHANDLES

It comes as a surprise to many that camping families regularly enjoy the same menus they relish at home, barring, of course, leg of lamb, roast turkey, and TV dinners—although the latter sometimes make a quick trip from a nearby country supermarket to a campground picnic table, via a Coleman oven.

This isn't quite as outlandish as it may seem when you consider that, in hopping from campground to campground, family campers daily pass supermarkets. Too, many camping areas maintain small food stores. Thus, the need for toting large quantities of specialized—and expensive—foods is eliminated. In addition, cleverly designed portable camp kitchens and modern camp refrigeration have simplified meal preparation. The camp cook no longer needs to work with pots and kettles precariously balanced on a rock fireplace, nor does he have to store perishables in a nearby creek to preserve them. Life in the woods, especially for the beginner, is far more gracious than it used to be.

A basic cooking kit can be assembled from household utensils, of course—a frying pan, one or two kettles, coffee pot, saucepan, mixing bowl, plus the many accessory items as useful in camp as they are at home—an egg beater, spatula, mixing spoon, and measuring cup, to name but a few. And, if economy is a factor, utensils borrowed from the kitchen will do the job nicely on a campstove. However, camp utensils are quite inexpensive, and they will save household equipment from abuse (a few dents are inevitable in camp) and soiling, or loss.

Aluminum nesting cook kits come to mind first. They usually consist of two or three kettles ranging from two to eight quarts, with covers that double as frying pans, dinner plates, plastic drinking cups, and sometimes tableware. We've found the kettles ideal for stews and soups (and berry picking), but their covers are suitable only as such—not as frying pans.

An acceptable redeeming feature among these combination cover/frying pan utensils is Teflon lining—not perfect—but a vast improvement over the bare aluminum cooking surfaces that develop hot spots and scorch foods. Nonstick sprays such as Pam are helpful, but if you're a serious camp cook, you'll use aluminum only for dishes with a high liquid level—soups, stews, or poached eggs! Aluminum is suitable for baking, too—a muffin tin, for example. But when it comes to frying or pan broiling, there is no more abominable utensil than an aluminum frying pan, even if it does double as a kettle cover! The plastic cups are an improvement over aluminum cups, which used to be included, and which burned lips from Maine to California because they conduct heat so effectively. But the plastic cups are little improvement. I detect a "polyethylene taste" in my coffee. Imaginary or not, plastic ruins coffee, according to my taste buds! Stainless steel is somewhat gentler on the lips, but best of all is enamelware. It conducts heat reluctantly and its vitreouslike surface is easy to clean, but it does chip. This is enamelware's weakness, but for the sake of coffee that tastes as coffee should, I'm willing to forgive this shortcoming.

Much the same can be said for aluminum

Ideal for campstove cooking, this cook kit has Teflon-lined utensils. ZEBCO

dinner plates supplied in most cook kits. We've acquired three or four nesting kits over the years, and part of the "breaking in" process calls for discarding the plates. Inevitably their high heat conductivity leaves a meat patty lodged solidly in a base of hardening grease long before the meal is eaten. We use enamelware or plastic plates, instead. We've come to the conclusion that nesting cook kits are little more than a source of kettles and covers.

The busiest utensil in camp is the frying pan, also referred to as a "skillet," and in the Maine woods, as a "spider." We use three different sizes of "old-fashioned" press-steel fry pans— 6, 9, and 12 inches in diameter. These are inexpensive (in country stores; not in city outlets, where they are virtually unknown), lightweight,

The mainstay of many an expert camp chef, the cast-iron skillet. GRISWOLD

tough, and best of all, they distribute heat evenly.

Even better are cast-iron skillets. These hold heat longer and more evenly and, the more they are used, the better flavor they impart to food.

They're available in the conventional round style, but search a little farther for the 9"-square type. Two of these fit perfectly, side by side, atop the larger Coleman or Thermos 2-burner stoves. Their square surfaces afford about 25 per cent greater cooking area than their round counterparts. They are quite heavy, I'll grant, but this is of little consequence to car campers. New cast-iron utensils require "seasoning," in addition to the factory "preseasoning" mentioned on the label. Otherwise, food takes on some of the iron flavor. Seasoning calls for greasing the utensil lightly with unsalted grease such as lard, then allowing it to stand at room temperature or in a low oven until the grease is absorbed into the iron. This should be repeated several times before the utensil is used. Thereafter, each use will improve it. Washing it with a detergent will remove this seasoning. Use only a mild soap and hot water to wash, and then only when absolutely necessary. Most woods cooks merely wipe theirs out with a clean cloth.

Most coffee pots supplied with nesting kits are satisfactory, although they may not be equipped with a percolator basket. Most family campers— and their consumption of coffee keeps South America happy and prosperous—seem to prefer

The author's car-camping cook kit. RIVIERE

conventional household percolators for use on campstoves. My favorite has a wide base, tapering sides, friction-fit cover, and a bail handle, with a ring or second handle at the base opposite the pouring spout. By means of the bail and the lower ring or handle, you can lift the pot and pour coffee with a pair of small forked sticks without touching the pot with your hands. (The TV cowboy who reaches into the fire with his bare hand for the coffee pot either drinks cold coffee or he has asbestos fingers.) The wide bottom hurries the heating of the water and

affords greater stability. When I worked as a guide in the Maine woods we used to have "tin knockers" make such coffee pots to our specifications, but to my delight Wearever produced an almost perfect replica a few years ago, complete with percolator basket and a cover that doesn't fall off when coffee is poured. There's no reason, of course, why a drip-type pot can't be used in camp. As a matter of fact, drinkers of instant coffee can do away with the pot altogether, heating water in a kettle.

Mixing bowls have many uses in camp (as

serving dishes or for salads), but the crockery type is subject to breakage. Some years ago we found a nesting set of three aluminum bowls in a Minneapolis department store. These are still in use, but we've never again seen them on sale. We've found stainless-steel bowls, but these are unnecessarily expensive for camping. We later discovered that northern Minnesota guides use metal bowls that they aptly call "dish-ups."

Several of the camp cooks whose products I most enjoy eating use pressure cookers over campstoves. Meal production time is minimized (fresh green beans in four minutes, corn on the cob in five); flavor, vitamins, and mineral salts are retained; and even mediocre cuts of meat are tenderized and their flavor concentrated. The words "pressure" and "steam" detract somewhat from the appeal the pressure cooker might have for many camp cooks. However, there's no need for apprehension. The pressure cooker is equipped with an automatic safety valve or fuse, which frees excess steam safely. Even this is a rare occurrence. Recently I "met" one whose safety valve hadn't "popped" in seventeen years of use. Detailed instruction booklets are included with new cookers, along with a wide variety of suggested recipes for camp meals.

The camping family that has a taste for freshly baked cake, pies, muffins, or biscuits will keep a Coleman oven busy. This is a boxlike unit, collapsible, with a heat indicator and a "peek" window, that operates atop a single burner. It may be used with propane fuel or gasoline, although leaded gasoline should be avoided. Remarkably efficient and easy to use, it will rescue you from the monotony of "store-bought" bakery goods.

Toast on a green stick over glowing coals is fun, there's no denying it, but who wants to wait for campfire coals in order to have breakfast? For many years we've used a "teepee" toaster, a four-sided metal pyramid that sits over a stove burner. At best it's a mediocre rig. Far better toast is possible more quickly with a "Camp-A-Toaster,"[1] an adaptation of the coffee-can toaster we made as youngsters in scouting. Two models are available: one square for a single slice, another rectangular for two slices. Over a propane or gasoline stove burner either produces superb toast.

I once took a fishing trip deep into the Ontario wilderness with a partner who insisted on toting a heavy, cast-iron griddle. Since he was so fond of it, I allowed him to carry it over the portages. In fact, I don't think he would have trusted me with it. However, whenever we camp by automobile we never fail to take along our "Old Eight-Pounder." It fits perfectly over both burners of our campstove, and its large cooking surface is ideal for the mass production of pancakes, bacon, sausage, hot dogs, even hamburgers. Insist upon cast iron, however. Magnesium alloys or aluminum griddles are subject to the same "hot spots" as the kettle-cover frying pans. Too, they sometimes warp.

Basic camp cooking will satisfy the needs of those to whom meals in camp are merely three-times-a-day incidentals. However, the cook who seeks new culinary adventures will probably investigate campfire cooking. Initial attempts at this should be on an experimental basis and not conducted when the family members have just returned from a seven-mile hike to the summit

[1] See the Appendix.

The best of all toasters for use on a campstove. CAMP-A-TOASTER

of Slidedown Mountain. Plan your first tries over a cookfire for less critical occasions, when a failure or delay won't endanger family harmony or your stature as a cook.

The most versatile cookfire utensil is the cast-iron Dutch oven. It can serve as a kettle for stews, soups, or one-pot meals to which it lends uniquely toothsome flavor; as a skillet; and as a baker or oven. For bean-hole beans, it's the perfect pot! I knew a pack-trip cook who also used his Dutch oven as a dishpan, but he also beat his wife and, as a boy, repeatedly pushed his grandmother down the cellar stairs. The campfire Dutch oven has three short legs so that it can be placed over a bed of glowing hardwood coals, and a rimmed cover upon which can be heaped a mixture of hot coals and ashes, the latter to keep the coals from burning out too rapidly. Versatile as it is, however, the Dutch oven is at its best as a baker, the heavy iron heating evenly and holding this heat well. If you're in doubt about judging its interior temperature, place an oven thermometer in it. Lifting the cover—best done with a forked stick—to check the heat range doesn't slow this oven. You'll have no trouble during your initial attempts at Dutch-oven baking if you confine yourself to easy-to-bake muffins, biscuits, or corn bread. With a little experience, roasts, pies, and cakes are the next steps toward your doctorate in campfire cooking. At any rate, you'll never lack for company at your picnic table. Incidentally, household Dutch ovens without legs and equipped with domed covers are not well suited to open-fire cooking, although they may be used on campstoves.

Even more fun to use is the reflector oven,

which dates back prior to 1800 and has never gone completely out of style, although it did hibernate for several generations as a woods cook's means of providing hot saleratus biscuits to early log drivers. The reflector oven uses reflected heat from an open fire, the flames "licking up" to the height of the oven. This heat "bounces" off the upper and lower sloping walls onto food placed on a shelf in the oven. Adjusting temperature is a matter of moving the oven closer to, or farther away from, the fire. Anyone doubting the efficiency of such a seemingly crude arrangement would have been amazed at a series of tests I conducted a few years ago during which we recorded 600 degrees in a Sims reflector oven before a fire of red oak. The fun of reflector-oven baking is that you can watch your biscuits rising and browning. One of my favorites is johnnycake, baked in an antique cast-iron gem tray, which we often enjoy with bean-hole beans.

A highly polished oven is more effective than a darkened or rusted reflector, but maintaining this polish requires a greater output of energy than I care to dispense, so I line the interior sloping walls with aluminum foil. Aluminum ovens are probably the most efficient. However, I have a battery of five, including a four-foot giant, made of metals that include tinned iron, aluminum, steel, and galvanized iron. With a lining of aluminum foil, any one is as efficient as the other. One type that falls short of these,

Griddle used atop a 2-burner stove will produce a complete meal for 4 to 5 persons. PAULIN

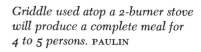

For the campsite gourmet cook, the cast-iron Dutch oven. RIVIERE

however, is a collapsible model without sides, these omitted for compactness when folded. When the wind blows, much of the heat from the fire escapes before it reaches the food. However, here again, aluminum foil comes in handy, when draped as temporary sides. Like our coffee pots in days gone by, we used to have reflector ovens made by local tinsmiths, but several styles are now available commercially, most of them folding types. The various ovens in my battery, for example, come from Maine, Colorado, Sweden, and Wyoming. My four-foot "shed baker," however, is homemade. There seems to be little commercial demand for a camping oven capable of eight dozen biscuits at one baking.

Another utensil popular with cooks who know their way around a cookfire is the basket broiler, originally designed for use *over* charcoal or a wood fire. It has been adapted by some, though, to broil meats (particularly steaks, chops, and hamburgers) in a vertical position, close to the side of the fire rather than over it. If placed horizontally in the conventional position, the juices and fats, which contain much of the meat's flavor, have only the thickness of the cut to run through before dropping into the fire. By plac-

ing the broiler vertically, these must run through the width or length of the slice before dropping. Hence, flavor loss is minimized. Some fats and juices are lost even in the vertical position, of course, but these can be salvaged by wrapping aluminum foil about the bottom of the broiler to form a drip pan. The drippings may then be used for basting or as a base for gravy.

Aluminum foil is popular with family campers, many of whom learned to use it as a means of cooking over glowing coals while in scouting. There is no end to the combinations of foods that can be cooked together, tightly wrapped in double layers of heavy-duty foil to minimize the danger of punctures. Actually, aluminum foil wrapped about food in this manner is, in effect, a miniature pressure cooker, sealing in all of the goodness of meats and vegetables. Most popular are simple meals, such as hamburger, vegetables, and potatoes, but we have friends who frequently roast a four-pound eye-of-the-round roast in foil. There are numerous booklets available that describe techniques and offer numerous recipes, these offered by manufacturers of foil.

We use foil a great deal, too, but find it diffi-

The basket broiler is ideal for campfire broiling; it catches drippings and minimizes drying out of meat. RIVIERE

cult to dispose of. It's practically indestructible and seemingly lasts forever if cast out into the woods, as so many thoughtless persons do. One trick that will aid disposal where rubbish cans are not available is to lay flat sheets over the flames of the campfire. This will "burn" the foil into a small glob.

When it comes to camp menus, family campers are fortunate. Depending upon how much time you want to devote, virtually every meal possible at home can be prepared over a campstove—barring, of course, a Thanksgiving turkey or a leg of lamb. (Even these can be done in a reflector oven.) As a result, campsite eating need not be spartan. A campstove will accommodate the same utensils you use at home: a skillet, kettle, coffee pot, griddle, double boiler, etc. And you can prepare the same type of meals.

Camping experts have cried out against the weight of canned goods for years. But if you're toting the food supply in the family car, does this weight really matter? Only rarely. In addition, supermarkets offer good eating in a dozen forms—many of them of the "instant" category. For example, the various instant soups can be embellished by combining two or more, possibly adding rice or barley. Prepared mixes of all sorts are on the shelves, as appropriate in camp as they are at home—biscuit, pancake, cornbread. Plus the combination canned/instant meals —Chinese dishes, spaghetti, and macaroni and cheese, to name only a few. Envelopes of powdered lemonade, tea, and grape and raspberry drinks need only the addition of water.

If you're carrying a portable ice chest of some sort, fresh meats are available en route from campground to campground, plus vegetables from roadside stands.

Good foods are universally distributed through supermarkets everywhere, and prices vary only slightly from one part of the country to another. So why load up a hundred pounds of grub at your home market? Unless you're headed for a remote area where foodstuffs are unavailable or likely to be excessively expensive, carry only two or three days' supply. Bring only the major staples from home.

Of course, as you acquire experience over a campstove, you may want to explore the wonders of fry-pan bannock or a hunter's stew slowly simmered over a campfire. Until then, take advantage of the supermarket and your campstove.

Chapter 13

COMFORT AT NIGHT

SLEEPING BAGS

Buying a sleeping bag for the first time can be a puzzling experience. I suppose it's a basic precept of modern packaging and merchandising, but the poorest-quality sleeping bag invariably bears the gayest and most colorful label, one that implies that the bag is just the thing for a weekend atop Mount McKinley or a fortnight in Baffin Land. Disappointment and chilblained feet usually follow. This, however, needn't be so.

The first step toward comfort at night while camping is to understand that a sleeping bag does not make you warm. It simply slows the escape of natural body warmth and, to accomplish this, a sleeping bag is padded with a "filler," which acts as an insulator.

In Chapter 1, the discussion of tent fabrics pointed out that the human body gives off moisture known as "insensitive moisture," which must pass out through a tent fabric, even while it repels rain. A sleeping bag filler and its outer shell have a similar dual role. Along with retaining body warmth, they must permit the outward passage of this moisture. Otherwise, a damp, clammy bedroll results.

Then we run into the matter of "loft," a term frequently used in describing backpackers' sleeping bags but rarely in family-camping literature. Yet it is vital. "Loft" is simply "fluffiness," the ability of a compressed material to expand, thus creating dead-air space which traps warmth. Loft is usually expressed as thickness. In other words, the greater the loft, the greater the thickness, the greater the insulation value, hence the greater the comfort. Family-camping sleeping bags are usually described as containing a given number of pounds of filler, such as "three pounds of 'Super-Therm Bagfil.'" Such a sleeping bag may be next to useless if the "Super-Therm" does not "loft" or expand suitably when the bag is unrolled. Another, filled with only two pounds of "Beddy-Bye Fibers," may be less bulky when rolled, and superbly comfortable because the "Beddy-Bye Fibers" "loft" or expand adequately.

Goose down is the most easily compressed of all sleeping bag fillers. And it provides the greatest loft per pound. In fact, 1 ounce of goose down may loft, or expand, to 500 cubic inches of insulation. A goose-down sleeping bag suitable for temperatures far below freezing can be compressed into a package barely larger than a football, yet when rolled out will loft to 2-inch or more thickness. And it is literally "light as a feather," since down is a "fuzz" obtained from the breasts of geese.

It has two drawbacks, however. The first is cost: For $50 you'll get a poor excuse for a sleeping bag. A good one will be priced at $80 upward—mostly upward, even up to $150. If you're thinking of outfitting your family of six, I've just soured you on down-filled sleeping bags! The second shortcoming really isn't critical unless you fall overboard and use your sleeping bag as a life preserver. A soaked down-filled sleeping bag will mat and take forever to dry, unless gently tumbled in a drier. Users of goose-down bags know this and are careful to avoid getting them wet.

Until recently, no manmade filler even approached the adaptability of goose down. This is no longer true. The E. I. Du Pont de Nemours Company has been whittling away at this challenge for years. I recall a campfire chat with a Du Pont engineer back in 1963 when we discussed the possibility of a "synthetic down" that would compress and loft as well as natural down. The engineer shook his head ruefully. "We're working on it," he said. "Maybe we'll do it, someday."

Up until that time, Du Pont had produced a polyester fiber that it marketed as "Dacron 88," its insulation characteristics excellent, its cost low, and its ability to pass off body moisture quite good. But it could not be compressed as tightly as down. A Dacron 88 sleeping bag was bulky.

Persistence apparently pays off. The new Polyester Fiberfill II may put down-producing geese out of business. Not immediately—but it's only a matter of time.[1]

Using equal weights of goose down and Fiberfill II, and compressing with equal pressure, a Fiberfill II sleeping bag will compress about 90 per cent as well as a down bag. In other words, if a down bag compresses to a 10-inch diameter, the Fiberfill II bag will compress to 11 inches.

Compressibility is one thing, but how about loft? After all, this is what retains body warmth and makes for comfort. It takes about 1.4 pounds of Fiberfill II to equal the loft or thickness of 1 pound of prime goose down. In bags of the same outer fabric and construction, a 2-pound down bag could be replaced by a 2.8-pound Fiberfill II bag.

A Fiberfill II bag absorbs less than 1 per cent moisture when dunked or exposed to a downpour. It retains its shape and loft. Down, on the other hand—as I've pointed out—will mat or

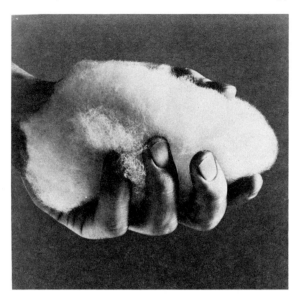

Dacron Polyester Fiberfill II, a new type of filler for sleeping bags and garments, rivaling the efficiency of down. DU PONT

lump, lose its insulation value, and take forever to dry.

Now for the body moisture problem. I own nine sleeping bags—some down, some of the old-style Dacron 88, and one new Fiberfill II type. My down bags are superb but costly. Some clamminess is felt in my older polyester bags. But the Fiberfill II feels as dry in the morning as my best down bag.

Up to this point, Fiberfill II has almost, but not quite, matched the general efficiency of goose down. At the risk of sounding like an advertising copywriter, take a look at cost. For about $30 you can buy a Fiberfill II sleeping bag that is 90 per cent as efficient as a $100 goose-down bag.

Your choice, then, is simplified. If you're planning extensive backpacking trips, and you have the financial resources, goose down is still the ultimate. But if yours is an average camping family headed for a series of weekend jaunts, plus an annual two-week car-hopping vacation, Fiberfill II is an economical, practical choice.

Other types of sleeping bag fillers are on the market, touted under various brand and trade names, but none of these—with the previously noted exception of PolarGuard—even remotely approaches down or Fiberfill II.

Sleeping bags insulated with polyurethane

---

[1] At the time of this writing there has also appeared PolarGuard, a product of the Celanese Corporation of America. This new insulating agent challenges Du Pont's Fiberfill II as the best synthetic insulator. Controversy currently exists among experts as to which is best. Some claim that PolarGuard is more stable, less inclined to shift, than Fiberfill II. Others disagree, and claim Fiberfill II to be superior. At any rate, most of the comments that I make in this chapter with regard to Fiberfill II can also be applied to PolarGuard. Frankly, at this point, I'm not sure which is superior.

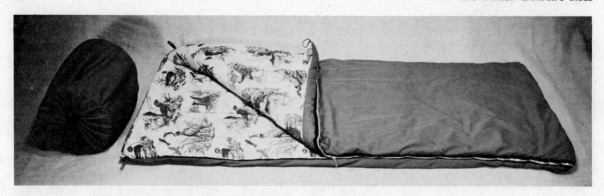

A family-camping-type sleeping bag insulated with Fiberfill II. LAACKE AND JOYS

foam have gained some publicity in recent years, but frankly, they are a "gimmick" seeking a niche in the marketplace. To roll one into its carrying bag, one almost needs a hydraulic press. Unrolled, they are stiff, with none of the soft resiliency of down or Fiberfill II bags.

Depending upon how much camping you do, you will sooner or later come up with a sleeping bag that needs cleaning or washing. Down bags usually require dry-cleaning, and not many professional dry cleaners are enthusiastic about this kind of business. Down bags can be washed by laying them out in a bathtub in a Woolite solution, gently stirring them, then drying them by tumbling gently in a drier. Fiberfill II bags, on the other hand, may be washed in a household or coin-operated machine, then tumble-dried.

Whatever bag you buy, don't take too literally the so-called thermal or warmth ratings. These are simply guidelines. Your metabolism rate (the ability of your body to generate heat), what you had for supper before retiring, exposure to wind or heat radiation while asleep, all of these will affect your sleeping bag's actual rating.

Although there can be no arbitrary rule, where nighttime temperatures do not drop much below 50 degrees, a 2-pound polyester bag may be suitable. In the northern states and in southern Canada (except at high altitudes, of course), 3 pounds are generally acceptable to a "warm sleeper," and a "cold sleeper" will want 4 pounds, possibly 5.

The outer wrapper or shell in family-camping sleeping bags is usually poplin or duck, the latter found in the better bags. Poplin, however, is excellent, although not as durable as duck. Cheap bags, generally in the $5 to $10 price range, often are equipped with a plastic or rubberized bottom usually touted as a "built-in ground cloth." This is a misguided sales gimmick, which deserves to remain on the dealer's shelf until doomsday. A waterproof panel, even on the bottom, prevents the escape of some body moisture so that such a bag becomes damp and clammy. If the bag is to be used on the ground without an air mattress, it should be laid on a separate, waterproof, ground cloth.

Low- and medium-priced sleeping bags are usually lined with outing flannel, its fuzzy nap being pleasant to the touch. Campers sometimes complain that, since flannel clings tenaciously to flannel, they find themselves hamstrung in their own night clothes if these too are flannel. However, most find the material more than satisfactory. More expensive sleeping bags, though, are likely to be lined with sateen, nylon, or similarly smooth or silky fabric.

A removable liner has notable advantages. Attached by means of tie tapes or snaps, such a liner may be of sheeting, cotton flannel, or—for extra warmth—wool blanketing. It can be removed for washing or dry-cleaning, thus eliminating the need for dry-cleaning the entire bag. Not only will a liner help keep the sleeping bag clean, but in the case of a wool liner, such as a blanket, it increases the bag's efficiency. If wool "scratches," a muslin or even percale sheet may be attached to the side of the blanket coming in contact with the body. Such liners can easily be added to sleeping bags lacking them by any camping mother or wife who's adept with a needle and thread.

When shopping for a sleeping bag, don't be influenced by the picturesque canopy rigged with forked sticks and shown in so many catalogs. No one has yet devised a means of crawling into such an arrangement, short of squirming into the bag from the foot end and closing the zipper by means of a six-foot cord. Actually the canopy serves well as a wrapper for the sleeping bag when rolled up—but for little else. Rigging the canopy with forked sticks for advertising purposes implies that the bag can be used for sleeping out of doors without shelter. No sleeping bag should be waterproof. Body moisture must be allowed to escape.

A hood, however, is another matter. This is designed to fit snugly about the head and shoulders, cutting off cool night air that might seep in or—more accurately—preventing the escape of body warmth. Some of these hoods are little more than flannel wrappers, but others are padded like the rest of the bag. A puckerstring draws the hood about the face for cold-weather comfort.

The "air mattress pocket" is frequently highlighted in sleeping bag advertising, usually by copywriters who have never been camping. If they had, they would know that when an air mattress is inflated within such a pocket, there's little room left in the sleeping bag for persons such as myself, who possess some degree of rotundity about the midriff. Some ads even boast of "two air mattress pockets." In the case of very slender persons or young children, using the pocket is feasible, but the average husky adult male will find it a snug fit, which makes rolling over a struggle. I prefer to lay my sleeping bag directly atop the mattress, although there's the risk of slipping or rolling off onto the hard ground during the night.

Sleeping bag zippers may be subject to considerable stress when you turn or twist in the bag, possibly driving a knee or an elbow into the slide fastener. If buying a bag, choose one equipped with a heavy-duty die-cast metal zipper—a No. 7 is excellent—or one of the newer nylon styles that are proving remarkably durable. Too, the zipper should run the length of the bag and across the bottom. Thus the bag can be fully opened for airing, and if you buy two alike, they can be "zipped" together to form a double sleeper.

Inside the sleeping bag and along the zipper's inner surface should be a "weather stripping" or baffle panel of insulated material to prevent the escape of warmth through the metal or nylon teeth. Better sleeping bags have such strips 3″ to 4″ wide and 1″ to 1½″ thick.

"Standard" sleeping bags are rectangular and about 34″×76″, adequate for most persons during the summer season. More portly campers, or those expecting extremes in weather, can buy "king size" models, up to 48″ wide and 96″ long. Smaller versions are available for children, too, usually 30″×54″, but regrettably these are often inadequately insulated, being marketed as "bargains."

Mummy-type bags, shaped roughly to conform to the contours of the human body, are lighter in weight and less bulky, and hence are preferred by backpackers. But they are more costly and somewhat restrictive. A restless sleeper will find his movements restrained by the bag. For family camping, the rectangular bag is more comfortable.

Sleeping bags require surprisingly little care beyond common-sense precautions. Generally they are warmer if "fluffed"—to increase the loft —before retiring. Down bags should be stored open and in a horizontal position. They should not remain rolled or tightly compressed through the winter, for example. Manmade fibers withstand compressing better than does down, but even these are better off for horizontal, open storage. Should a sleeping bag become wet or damp, don't hesitate to toss it into a coin-operated drier, with the heat turned to low range. Not only will this dry it well, but it will also restore loft or "fluff." For sanitary reasons sleeping bags should be aired daily in good weather, preferably in sunlight, but take them back inside before the sun drops. Otherwise, evening dampness or dew will make them clammy.

CAMP BEDS

Camp cots have a well-deserved reputation as chilly accommodations. As warm air rises, cold air reaches the sleeper from underneath. Even a top-quality down bag, used on a cot, may prove inadequate in relatively mild weather. You may have two inches of loft over and along the sides of your body, but underneath, your weight may compress the down to a mere quarter inch. Obviously, body warmth escapes easily through this thin barrier. The old-style polyester was superior to down in this respect,

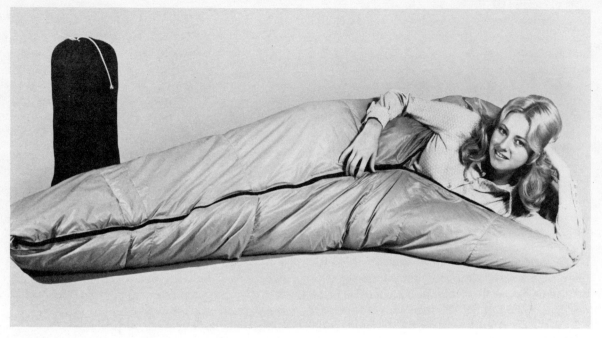

A mummy-type sleeping bag, also insulated with Fiberfill II. COLEMAN

in that it did not compress as readily. It remained efficient even under the weight of a heavy camper. Polyester Fiberfill II, however, having almost achieved the desirable characteristics of down, is also subject to the compressibility shortcoming. Both down and Polyester Fiberfill II need additional insulation underneath whether used on a cot or on the ground.

This calls for an air mattress or a foam pad. Camping trailers often are equipped with foam mattresses ranging from 4 to 6 inches thick. Foam of that thickness cannot be rolled compactly, so tenters must settle for thinner pads. Backpackers are offered foam pads barely 1¼ inches thick and only 48 inches long. I've used such a pad. It was like sleeping on the sports page of *The Wall Street Journal!* A more realistic pad, 2½ inches thick and 75 inches long, is available. It provides not only adequate insulation but sufficient cushioning to remove sleeping

Two sleeping bags "zipped" together for use as a double.
LAACKE AND JOYS

out from the torture category. However, it's bulky, and rolling it tightly is like putting a collar on a wet eel.

An air mattress seems like the ideal solution. Deflated, it's compact; properly inflated, it's comfortable; it's reasonably priced. But it, too, has shortcomings. It does not insulate as well as foam, and most models take until the middle of next week to deflate. This calls for opening the valve as soon as you awaken and allowing the mattress to lie flat until everything else has been packed into the car. By that time the struggle to expel trapped air will have been minimized, but by no means eliminated completely.

Nevertheless, an air mattress may be a better choice than a foam pad, in the case of limited space aboard the family car. Four foam pads will occupy close to six cubic feet; four air mattresses, barely one-half cubic foot.

The better air mattresses are made of rubberized cotton. Considered best, because it most closely approximates a bed mattress, is the tufted type. The next-best choice is the "I-beam" tubular construction model, so called because the walls of individual tubes when seen from one end resemble a steel construction beam. This is only slightly removed from the comfort of the tufted mattress, but its cost may be about half. Poorest choice of all is plastic. I've tried two of these. One failed the first night. The other lasted longer—three nights, in fact. By the way, don't allow children to use rubberized-cotton air mattresses as play rafts while swimming. This causes rapid deterioration of the fabric, and sudden deflation in deep water might bring tragedy.

Don't be surprised if your "30-inch" air mattress shrinks to 24 inches in width when inflated. This is normal.

Inflating an air mattress by mouth is tedious and hard on the lungs. This was a chore assigned to our two youngsters until they presented me on my birthday with an air mattress pump. Several styles are available, including a bellows type activated by foot pressure, a rubber bulb that is squeezed by hand, and a metal cylindrical pump. In keeping with space-age camping, there's an electrically powered pump that operates from the car's cigarette lighter—an increasingly versatile automotive accessory, indeed. Beware of a pump built into the air mattress. I have such a mattress stored somewhere in the clutter over the garage. Someday I'll prob-

The beauty of synthetic-filled sleeping bags, they can be washed. COLEMAN

ably take it to the dump, but in the meantime I've been hoping that someone will devise some means of repairing the broken pump without having to cut open the mattress.

An overinflated air mattress is no more comfortable than bare ground or a board floor. Often, in testing for proper inflation, a camper will kneel on the mattress or press his fist into it, and naturally this concentration of pressure at one or two points gives the impression that the mattress is too soft. Test the mattress by lying on it. Your body should sink into it slightly but not enough so that you feel the ground underneath. Of course, if you prefer a hard bed, inflate it until you attain the desired firmness.

Air mattresses are best stored by hanging or laying them flat in a warm, dry room. Extreme heat or cold is detrimental to them. If you lack space for storage in this manner, roll them loosely. Never fold so that creases form.

One type of camp cot that eliminates the need for both the foam pad and the air mattress is one that has a batt of polyester or down sewed to its underside. This insulation can't be compressed by the sleeper's weight. Such cots are relatively costly; $42 for a goose-down insulated cot (as I write this) and $32 for one padded with polyester. However, there's no reason why a camping wife or mother can't sew a Dacron batt to the bottom of each of the family camp cots at a substantial savings.

Old-time car campers think of a camp bed as an "army cot," the still-available wooden-legged model that invariably develops a sway that leads to eventual collapse. Too, the legs of such cots may gouge holes in canvas floors. However, they are the least expensive of folding camp beds. On the market are several versions of steel- and aluminum-framed cots with W-shaped leg frames which, when inserted into the cot's horizontal bars, exert a powerful side thrust that keeps the cot open. When folded, these usually form a bundle about 3″×5″×38″. Steel models weigh about 15 pounds, aluminum about 7. The difference in quality lies not only in the metal parts but also in the canvas, which in better cots may be 12-ounce duck. Some models are only about 8″ high, ideal for low-walled tents. On the other hand, there's little storage space under these. Our own family has five such cots, one insulated, two steel-framed, and two aluminum types, and in the aggregate they've logged well over a thousand nights of use and are still in excellent condition.

The double-deck cot is highly practical. These are usually aluminum-framed and weigh about 16 pounds. Some can be separated for use as two single cots. They are ideal for use in cottage tents where floor area may be at a premium while wall height is going to waste. The upper bunk in most models is only about 30″ from the floor, but for stability the heavier sleeper should be in the bottom bed. Children particularly like these.

BLANKETS

Blankets have pretty well passed out of the camping picture, but where budget limitations prevent sleeping bag purchases, by all means use blankets. However, don't take along household castoffs as "good enough for camping." The only blankets that qualify for camp use are the best all-wool blankets in your home. For average summer nights, two 3-pound blankets usually will do. Three or even four will be needed on cool nights. A sleeping bag of blankets can be made by overlapping at least two blankets so that there are two layers over and two under the sleeper. Open edges can then be pinned together with "horse blanket pins," available from many camping equipment outfitters. At best, though, this is an improvisation and rarely satisfactory on cold nights. I would prefer to forgo other camping gear in favor of buying sleeping bags.

Chapter 14

CLOTHING AND FOOTWEAR

Family camping is the least strenuous of the so-called "outdoors" sports. There are no treacherous peaks to scale or wild whitewater to run. You won't have to buck gale winds, plod into the teeth of a blizzard, or trudge weary miles under a heavy pack. You *can* undertake such expeditions while family camping, of course, but it's a rare family indeed that does.[1] Which means that you won't need expensive, specialized clothing. The chances are that you have a well-suited wardrobe hanging in the hall closet.

Between May and October in most parts of the country, sports clothing worn during typical suburban activities is completely in order. It pretty well boils down to wearing what you please, bearing in mind that clothes must also afford protection—against sun, rain, an occasional chilly evening, and insects.

Generally speaking, men, women, and children will find their regular wear-at-home underclothing fully adequate. With easy access to coin-operated laundries, either en route or in campgrounds, you can probably get along with two or three changes. The more you carry, of course, the fewer will be your visits to the laundry.

However, if your family enjoys preseason outings or likes to extend the season well into autumn, snow squalls and frosty mornings may require long underwear. Wool is warmest but "scratchy" on bare skin. In that case, invest in the double-fabric type: cotton next to the skin,

wool on the outside. Lightweight "fish net" underwear, popular with winter sports outdoorsmen, is also excellent.

There is no arbitrary rule regarding the choice of underwear. When you will want to shift from brief skivvies to long johns will depend on your activity, the latitude and altitude and, of course, the weather. In my country I've seen fourteen inches of snow on the tenth day of May, and shirtsleeve weather in mid-November. This is not unusual in many parts of the northern states.

In the outdoors, I wear wool socks all year-'round. They have a cushioning effect on the feet, and they help to counter both hot and cold weather. These are especially appropriate for camping, where most of us do a great deal more walking than at home or on the job. For lounging about the campsite, thin cotton socks may be suitable, but mosquitoes have little trouble piercing them. Medium-weight "athletic" socks are a good choice. During a Canadian trip last summer, I bought a half dozen pair of "wool" socks from the Hudson's Bay Company. Some ninety miles back in the bush I checked the label more carefully and discovered that they were part synthetic fibers. I'd no cause for complaint, however. They were superbly comfortable and durable during a tough trip.

Blue jeans are a sound choice for children. As most mothers know, they show little dirt even after a busy day of scampering through the woods or along the waterfront. They're tough, and tears are easily repaired. Adults frequently wear jeans too, or cotton work trousers. Tight-

---

[1] For suggestions on suitable clothing and equipment for such activities, see my *Backcountry Camping* (Garden City, N.Y.: Doubleday & Company, 1971).

fitting Levi's are miserable in camp because they bind. I doubt, though, that my recommendations will have any effect on teen-agers' penchant for pouring themselves into tightly shrunk pants. "Stretch slacks" for women, as well as regular slacks, are well suited to campground wear. Wool slacks, too, may be included in the wardrobe for cool evenings or stormy days. One heavy wool shirt or jacket for each member of the family will prove a wise investment for cool evenings. Wool should be closely and firmly woven, or else it will snag easily.

A sweater worn under a lightweight jacket of such material as poplin or nylon is a fine cool-evening combination, and better yet when the wind is blowing. For children, inexpensive sweatshirts may serve as well. In fact, many adults wear them too. The better outdoor clothing shops have a tremendous variety of women's wool jackets in attractive designs and colors, but they're often painful to the accompanying husband's pocketbook. Nevertheless, every camping wife or mother is entitled to one special jacket she particularly enjoys wearing for evening strolls or community campfires. Heavy jackets or mackinaws are seldom needed during the season when family campers are abroad, but if your family gets an early start in the spring, or if you extend your camping until it's time to shop for the Thanksgiving turkey, mackinaws are recommended. One feature that I personally like in all outer clothing is numerous and large pockets.

Such a wardrobe will pretty well prove ample for cool-to-cold summer weather, but what about the dog days of August, or the sultriness of June, even in the North? Shorts are in order. Permanent-press and drip-dry synthetics are a joy, whether shirts, blouses, slacks, or shorts. But here again, mosquitoes and black flies lick their chops at the sight of campers clad briefly in thin attire! Generous use of repellents is part of a hot-weather fashion show on almost all campgrounds. Cotton shirts and slacks repel insects better. In fact, I wear long-sleeved flannel shirts for hot-weather camping in the woods, although I admit to rolling up the sleeves during the heat of the day, depending upon a pipeful of Old Horsehair Aromatic Parlor Mixture to keep the bugs at bay.

As to footgear for adults, it's difficult to improve upon the low-cut moccasin with composition soles. These are light, tough enough to protect the feet, and they withstand considerable wetting; certainly they are more appropriate or "woodsy" than sandals. Open sandals, so comfortable for patio wear, should not be worn in camp, since they do not protect the feet against sharp rocks or stubs. Too, it'll be only a matter of minutes before both your socks and your feet will need a bath. Soleless or "Indian" moccasins are delightful for lounging, but because they lack heels, you'll find the muscles in the back of your legs aching if you walk extensively in them. They're best suited for canoeing. Six-to-ten-inch boots are frequently recommended, but these are out of place on well-beaten campground paths and roadways. They're for hiking in rough or rocky country. Even then, a six-inch boot is ample. Loafers, for men and women, are comfortable if no great amount of walking is planned.

Footgear for children is likely to consist of sneakers, and these are fine in good weather, but if it rains, wet feet are the order of the day. In this case, have the kids don the all-rubber or plastic slipover boots that they wear over their shoes on the way to school. They can then paddle in the puddles with immunity.

Suitable headgear is often overlooked. Never undertake a camping trip without some sort of

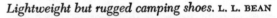

Lightweight but rugged camping shoes. L. L. BEAN

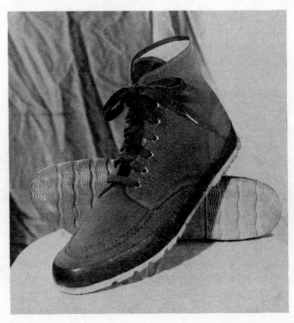

head covering for each member of the family. In the comfort of a tree-shaded campground you can leave it in the tent or camper, but when rain pelts the area, it's indispensable. And if you are active—even passively, such as fishing—under a hot sun, a hat of some sort is a must.

Probably the most popular piece of headgear is the visored cotton cap. It protects the wearer's eyes from the sun and will turn a light rain. In good weather, though, most campers prefer to go bareheaded—except the youngster who's just acquired a new cowboy hat. If the sun gets too hot, or rain sets in, I don a battered felt hat which, due to its age, the extent of its travels, and the fine fishing I've enjoyed under it, rates some degree of respect in our household. A felt hat is best worn in the rain with the crown punched up into a dome and with the brim turned down. This provides quick rain runoff. For women, the plastic scarves they wear in the rain are probably far more practical.

Even when insects are only moderately active, they have a knack of getting into women's hair. A thin nylon scarf tied under the chin protects against them.

Rainwear is the only item of family camping apparel that may require some degree of specialization. Fashionable city-type raincoats, designed solely to protect while the wearer is walking, are completely impractical. Few of them, too, will withstand a prolonged downpour without wetting through. You're supposed to duck into a doorway or hail a cab when the heavens unloose.

By far the best protection in camp is the poncho, little more than a flat sheet of rubberized material, coated nylon, or plastic, with a hole at its center through which you poke your head into a hood. Snaps close it at the sides. It fits loosely, provides ventilation, and allows freedom of movement without binding or buttons popping.

An alternate choice is the rain shirt, which drapes over the wearer like a small tent, covering even the feet if you're seated. It's a little difficult to climb into, though, and may prove too warm if you exercise. The choice of children's raingear boils down to front-buttoning raincoats or ponchos. If children are old enough to be in scouting, chances are they already own the latter. Children's rainhats are pretty much limited to "sou'westers," and these are excellent.

One style of raingear to avoid is the so-called "rain suit," consisting of plastic or rubberized-cotton trousers and a hooded parka. This was designed for protection while standing watch on World War II North Atlantic freighters, where personal activity was minimal. Used actively on a campground, it is a walking Turkish bath! What's more, it's a miserable rig to climb into and out of.

As for nighttime wear, the better the quality of your sleeping bag, the less critical is your choice. Flannel pajamas are the most widely accepted sleeping garments among family campers, although on a warm night, lightweight cotton (without flannel's "fuzziness" or nap) may prove more comfortable. For little tots, garments such as Denton sleepers are practical. Inexperienced campers, encountering cold nights with inadequate sleeping bags, often don daytime clothing for added warmth, the value of this probably more psychological than actual. However, sleep socks *are* effective, but don't wear them by day, as this wears off the nap and compresses the loft, cutting their warmth-retaining qualities. Set aside a special pair for night wear only.

This chapter is brief and contains no startling revelations regarding camp clothing for the simple reason that most camping families probably have suitable clothing on hand, not quite ready for discard and still useful as knock-about garb about the yard or patio. Keep in mind that you'll be traveling by car, not by canoe or on snowshoes, and that you'll be close to coin laundries. You needn't look like a state-aid case, but there's a good chance that the blue jeans you wear while mowing the lawn are just fine for family camping.

Chapter 15

TOTING AND SETTING UP

BEFORE LEAVING

"Toting" is the woods word for "carrying." Actually, family campers do little toting except possibly from a garage or attic storage space to the car, and again at the campground, from the car to the campsite, seldom more than a few feet. The family car, however, will be called upon to haul several hundred pounds possibly for thousands of miles. Some thought should be given to the manner in which gear and passengers are loaded.

Obviously the family car should be thoroughly checked before an extended trip—tires, battery, brakes, lights, turn signals, rear-view mirrors, transmission fluid, grease, and oil. It's so much simpler to make repairs at your regular service garage than along an expressway or remote country road. Tenters' cars especially are often overloaded. A car-top carrier can eliminate jamming camping equipment into the rear trunk or rear seat. This, too, helps keep the car on an even keel and makes it much easier to handle. Station wagons, especially, when heavily loaded in the rear, tend to handle like small boats in rough water, the "stern" weaving back and forth. If your car-top carrier is the removable type, set it as far forward as possible to increase stability. If there are youngsters in the family, load your equipment so that they have a place in which they can enjoy simple games, read books, or even take a nap. Remember that highway travel can be monotonous for them. They won't appreciate the scenery or roadside histori-

cal sites with the same enthusiasm as adults. Take along a variety of inexpensive games in a separate box, and hand these out as a series of "surprises" as the need arises. If your family is a large one, look into the feasibility of hauling a utility trailer for the camping gear, thus freeing all of the passenger space for comfortable traveling. Travel and tent trailer campers, of course, haul extra equipment in their trailers.

"Last in, first out" is the key to wise loading. Keep in mind that sandwiches for a noon luncheon en route should be easy to get at, not behind the outboard motor or back of the tent. If foods are to be warmed at a roadside stop, the campstove and fuel should be placed so that they can be reached without having to move other gear. This will save time.

In packing equipment and supplies, divide these into "departments," so that unloading and setting up camp is an orderly process, not chaos that involves searching for tent stakes in the toy box or the air mattress pump behind the spare tire. Departments may include:

Food: Should comprise all of the equipment and supplies related to the preparation of meals—the camp pantry, cooking kit, folding table, campstove, fuel, matches.

Shelter and Comfort: The tent, stakes, guy lines, canopy or dining fly, air mattresses, cots, lantern, tent heater, sleeping bags.

Clothing: Each member of the family old enough for this responsibility should look after his or her own clothing, although for compactness this may all be packed in one container. Old suitcases or ditty bags are ideal.

Personal Needs: Razor blades, shaving cream, suntan lotions, sunglasses, cold cream, hair rollers—in fact, all of the little necessities taken for granted at home, but which will be sadly missed on a campground if overlooked or mislaid.

Medical: The first-aid kit is obvious, of course, but how about special medications or prescription medicines that some members of the family may require?

Sports, Hobbies, Toys: Binoculars for the bird watcher; license and tackle for the fisherman; filters and film for the photographer; toys for the children.

During the excitement and confusion of planning and organizing the trip, don't forget installment or mortgage payments that may fall due while you're away. There may be a nasty demand notice plus a "late charge" billing in your mailbox when you return. Check the expiration dates of your credit cards, too. Trying to buy a tankful of gas with a credit card that expired three days ago can be embarrassing.

One last step remains before taking off on that high adventure: closing the home. Notify police that you'll be away so they can keep an eye on your property as they patrol the city. If you live in the country, report your coming absence to the sheriff or to the state police.

If you are leaving for an extended stay, disconnect all appliances. Don't just turn them off. A friend's TV caught fire while turned off but still plugged in! Pull the plug on the automatic washer and drier, television set, range, furnace, water heater, and refrigerator. To keep the latter sweet-smelling and to prevent mildew, use an old Navy trick: Spread a half pound of regular-grind coffee on the bottom shelf. Don't use instant coffee. It'll absorb moisture and turn to a gooey mess. Turn off the main water valve, too. Some youngster might open an outside spigot, and water will run until you return.

Notify the post office to forward mail or withhold deliveries. Advise the milkman and paper boy. An accumulation of bottles and newspapers on the porch is an invitation to burglary. Some like to leave a single light burning, usually in a bathroom, but this ruse is obvious to professional housebreakers, and even an amateur can read the meaning behind that same lonesome light burning night after night. Better protection is afforded by automatic devices, quite inexpensive, that turn lights on and off at preset times. Two or three of these in various parts of the house create the illusion of activity within. Attach one of these to the radio or tape player with the volume turned up moderately high. If you live in an apartment building, ask the superintendent to check your door and apartment daily. A small gratuity will usually gain the most hard-boiled super's co-operation.

Neighbors are often your best burglary or vandalism protection. If your neighbor has two cars, for instance, ask him to park one of them in your driveway. You can do the same for him when he goes on vacation.

Some cities have instituted a neighborhood crime watch. No night-riding vigilantes are involved. Neighbors simply keep an eye out for suspicious behavior, loitering strangers, or cars cruising by repeatedly at slow speeds, appraising the neighborhood's possibilities for an easy heist. The program is sponsored by police departments, and officers understand that an occasional false alarm may arise, but nonetheless they'll respond quickly to a call. If no such program exists in your city, it's a simple matter to organize one, even if it covers only your block.

If you have a garden, arrange for someone to care for it. Have someone mow the lawn if your trip is to be lengthy. Ask a neighbor to remove "throwaway" circulars, which may jam your mailbox or litter your porch. Leave an itinerary with a friend or relative so that you can be reached in case of emergency. Be sure that fire, burglary, and vandalism insurance policies are in force. Place valuables in a safe deposit box, and leave furs or expensive clothing in the care of a storage firm.

Under no circumstances announce in advance that you'll be away on a prolonged vacation. Small-town or county newspapers have local correspondents who are paid by the inch—the more detail, the more money. A notice from one of them to the effect that "Mr. and Mrs. Jeffrey Jones, and son John, and daughter Mary, will leave next Sunday for a thirty-day camping trip to Yellowstone . . ." is virtually an engraved invitation to burglary or vandalism. Some conscientious newspapers won't print this sort of notice, but others are more anxious to fill their news columns. If a "correspondent" calls you in advance of your trip for details, ask her (it's almost invariably a woman) to withhold the story until you return, assuring her of full details then.

Don't expect that these suggestions will burglarproof your home. Casual thieves and roaming vandals will generally be dissuaded by basic precautions, but the professional housebreaker knows all the tricks. But he rarely makes an overt move unless unqualified success is obvious. He is not a gambler. He likes a sure thing. Your best weapon against him is doubt, uncertainty. A changing pattern of lighting in the home, the sound of music, a car in the driveway—any of these will raise that doubt in his mind and quite likely send him farther down the street to case a darkened house.

ONCE YOU'VE ARRIVED

If you've made reservations for a campsite, it will be awaiting you, of course. Lacking a reservation, and if the camping area is not crowded, you may be allowed to inspect available sites and then make a choice. If this is the case, be sure to report back to the office immediately so that the manager will know which site you've chosen. Don't count on being able to do this at a popular campground during July or August, however. In this instance, you may be assigned a specific site.

As a family camper choosing a site in an organized campground, you won't face the rather complex problems of the wilderness camper who must appraise a piece of raw ground and decide whether or not it is practical. He has to be sure that his site won't flood during a sudden downpour, that dead trees don't endanger his camp, that a dominant tree won't invite lightning, or that poison ivy doesn't lurk. In a family campground, these problems have been eliminated. In fact, the area may even have been sprayed to rid it of insect pests. However, even in an area where individual sites have been more or less "standardized," you'll find some more desirable than others.

You'll want a scenic outlook, of course, either a countryside panorama, a view across the lake or river, or possibly the quiet and peace of dense woodlands. Consider, too, that a campsite bordering on a busy campground road will expose you to traffic noise and dust, to say nothing of danger to small tots. The boat dock, swimming beach, or playground are irresistible to children, but if you pitch your camp near any one of these, you may find the commotion hardly conducive to a restful vacation. On the other hand, you may prefer to camp near these facilities so that you can keep an eye on youngsters without leaving your site.

There is a trend among campgrounds, private and public, to reserve the waterfront as a community area, permitting camping only a hundred feet or so back from the lakeshore. However, many campgrounds still offer lakeshore sites, sometimes at premium fees. These are attractive, naturally, but if the shoreline drops off sharply, such a site may be hazardous to small children. Think twice before choosing a site in the vicinity of a comfort station. Such a site may seem ideal, at first glance, if children have to "make a visit" during the night, but bear in mind that practically all of the campers in this section will parade by your site. You'll enjoy all of the privacy of a department store window. Observe, too, whether or not sites are well spaced, with a green-growth barrier between them. It's nice to be neighborly, but not twenty-four hours a day and to the extent that you can peer into your neighbor's stew pot from your picnic table. Regrettably, some commercial areas, bent upon all possible revenue per acre, offer sites little larger than a Fifth Avenue lawn.

If you use a travel trailer, be sure the site spur is suitable for your rig. A tent trailer can generally be fitted into a site even if it entails maneuvering by hand, but a travel trailer will require jockeying with the car. A camper, staying in our area one night several years ago, insisted on backing his 22-foot trailer into an impossible site, finally wedging his unit against a beautiful yellow birch that I particularly prized. He threw a tantrum of no small proportions when I refused to cut the tree down. In freeing his trailer he damaged both it and the tree.

Almost invariably, campers place a tent or trailer with its door facing a lake or river. During good weather this is making the most of a site. However, on the shores of large lakes, where storm winds may rise to a ferocity that will peel the buffalo off a nickel, I prefer to face my shelter away from such an exposure so that winds

The National Park Service not only provides campsites, but its rangers can also be helpful with local information. NATIONAL PARK SERVICE

can "roll off the back" of a tent or trailer. You can always walk around the unit to enjoy the view.

Just as you would examine the neighborhood before buying a house, look over your next-site neighbors before deciding. Nine chances out of ten, they'll prove companionable and delightful company, but there's always the off-chance that you may pitch your camp next to a family battlefield, or expose yourself to juvenile mayhem. Unfortunately, there *are* a few families who are not particularly good neighbors, and the general "tone" or atmosphere about their site may give some hint of this.

Setting up camp can be a smooth and uncomplicated operation if a little planning goes into it. Most campers arrive late in the afternoon, and after the rush to set up the shelter, cook supper, and eat, they may find themselves doing dishes by lantern light while other campers are munching popcorn and swapping tales about their campfires. Sound organization calls for unloading the campstove, portable camp

kitchen, and the food supply, going for water—all before any attempt is made to erect the tent. This permits the cook to prepare the evening meal while the rest of the family is busy setting up, inflating air mattresses, placing cots, and unrolling sleeping bags. The cook shouldn't become involved in these chores. Asking her, or him, to hold a guy line while you drive a stake may result in scorched corn chowder. Respect the division of chores and, likely, supper will be done just as camp is pronounced ready for occupancy.

Naturally, such technique needn't apply to tent or travel trailer campers. Tent trailers with built-in cooking and dining facilities must, of course, be set up first. As for a travel trailer, once it's in place, there's little need for organization of camping chores.

Tenters and tent trailer campers should check the lantern before darkness sets in. It may require a new mantle, easier to install by daylight than in the darkness or by the light of a flickering match. If time permits before dark, you can then stroll about the area, locating "the facilities." This is a good time, too, to call on neighbors. When bedtime comes, you'll find yourself fully relaxed and your vacation under way just as you had planned it.

In seeking out a campground, bear in mind that three weekends invariably see a horrendous crush of traffic: Memorial Day, July Fourth, and Labor Day. If you plan to celebrate these holidays in camp, make a reservation weeks in advance. Even overflow areas and little-known campgrounds may be bulging with wall-to-wall tents and trailers.

The so-called "shortage" of campsites is not as acute as it has been portrayed, except during these three holidays. It makes little sense to demand that parks and private campgrounds gear their capacity to three weekends of peak business, running at 30 to 40 per cent of capacity the rest of the season.

The shortage of campsites in the United States has been grossly exaggerated. True, certain popular national and state parks, as well as some of the better private campgrounds, are well booked through July and August. But I've found that a friendly approach to a ranger, or private campground manager, often leads to information about little-known or uncrowded campsites close by. There's no guarantee, of course, but chances are that while well-known Blue Waters Campground is bulging with tents and trailers, nearby Icky Crick Campsite has tent space going begging, along with a beautiful view, remoteness, and peace and quiet. Don't be afraid to ask questions or to seek out more remote camping areas.

Chapter 16

PLANNING A TRIP

A little research in January can lead to the ultimate camping trip in July. But a haphazard "Let's load up an' go" departure on July 3 without prior planning is almost sure to be a disaster.

Whether you're headed for a specific area or on a roaming transcontinental trip, the first move is to write to the tourist promotion agencies[1] in those states through which you will pass. Some have soft-pedaled their tourist enticements, but most of them still supply colorful, informative literature. Gloss hurriedly over the standard clichés—"lakes teeming with fish" or "Huckinsville caters to your every wish." This is tourist-trap drivel, meaningless. However, buried in such pamphlets, casually mentioned, are local attractions that are little known nationally but worthwhile. As a logging buff, I was delighted to learn about logging museums in Rhinelander, Wisconsin, and at Patten, Maine, each with a superb replica of an old-time lumber camp, in humble local chamber of commerce-style pamphlets. Old home weeks, rodeos, flower festivals, water carnivals, art exhibits, canoe and boat races, various hobby exhibits, "open house" in colonial towns, Indian ceremonials, clam bakes and lobster festivals, shoo-fly pie picnics—you name it, there's a celebration for it somewhere. These rarely make network TV news, but they often afford a day's fun, a chance for strangers to become friends. New Hampshire discovers Iowa; Idaho gets a new look at Georgia. America's truly great attractions are not Old Faithful, the Grand Canyon, or Pike's Peak. People, their local customs, celebrations, cultures, and centennials are much more worthwhile experiences than standing in line to photograph Mount Rushmore!

On a more crassly practical note, advance study will reveal climate and weather expectancies. Rocky Mountain passes, climbing to ten thousand feet, may call for long underwear even in summer. Insects in the North Woods during early summer, high humidity in parts of the South, or devastating heat in the Southwest deserts all may call for rerouting or rescheduling a trip—providing you are forewarned.

Don't overlook maps during your planning. These not only may save unnecessary driving but may also reveal attractions such as fishing waters, ghost towns, isolated campgrounds, waterfalls, hiking trails, and fire towers—all possibilities for interesting side trips.

Hobbies, too, sometimes fit into camping trips. One of my travel "therapies" is visiting second-hand bookstores in search of camping books for my library. Collectors of minerals, botany samples, matchbook covers, or what-have-you can blend their pastimes with camping. Photographers and fishermen, of course, are in their element during a well-planned camping trip.

CAMPING LIBRARY

A camping library is a fascinating and enlightening off-season hobby. Not only do I collect books on the subject, but my shelves include

[1] See the Appendix.

complete files on several outdoor periodicals. I can't resist "Send the coupon NOW" appeals in advertising, so I receive veritable gold mines of information and suggestions from catalogs sent out by camping equipment dealers, mail-order firms, and manufacturers. A few charge a token fee "to cover cost of printing and mailing." I've always resented having to pay in order to read a businessman's advertising, but nonetheless the investment is usually worthwhile.

Highly pertinent information is available for the price of a postal request from the U. S. Forest Service, the National Park Service, the Bureau of Land Management, the U. S. Army Corps of Engineers, the Bureau of Indian Affairs, the various state park and forest departments, and state associations of campground owners. Timberland owners, pulp and paper companies, forestry, conservation, and wilderness organizations—all of these have invaluable information available for the asking.[2]

One source of information usually overlooked is the U. S. Government Printing Office. You can be placed on a free mailing list to receive the bimonthly *Selected U. S. Government Publications* bulletin. Each issue lists about a hundred publications, 95 per cent of which have little bearing on camping or the outdoors. But the remaining 5 per cent is invaluable, especially as the camping season approaches. Included are pamphlets describing in detail the various national parks and forests; a list of Indian tribes that operate campgrounds; or a $.10 booklet such as *How to Be Safe from Insects in Recreation Areas*. It is a rare bimonthly bulletin in which I find nothing of interest. To receive it, you merely have to request it.[3]

Other sources of information include automobile makers: Ford, Chrysler, General Motors, American Motors; the airlines (many run "camper specials"); and automobile clubs. Conservation organizations, too—such groups as the Wilderness Society, American Forestry Association, the Sierra Club, and the National Wildlife Federation—offer invaluable planning data.

A few well-directed postcards can make you the best-informed camper in your neighborhood. Clip an occasional coupon, too. For several years I've maintained four four-drawer office files jammed with data, and several hun-

dred soft- and hard-cover books, plus overflowing periodicals that I must cull frequently to avoid burial by paper. Camping is a substantial part of my livelihood, so I maintain files far more extensive than you're likely to need. A simple, one-compartment household-type file will probably suffice.

TRAVEL FILE

If this holds a dozen file folders, it will do away with the chaos of the glove compartment and the lost road map. Such files are available in department and discount stores. They'll hold not only road maps, but also campground reservations, instructions and parts lists for camp lantern and stove, campground directories, travel folders, a budget book for trip expenses, birth certificates (for a swing through Canada), an equipment checklist, insurance certificates, a booklet of favorite camp recipes, and other vital paper necessities.

CAMPGROUND DIRECTORIES

Campground directories range all the way from hand-out pamphlets to full-fledged hardbound books, most of them revised annually to keep pace with changes and to include new camping facilities, which continue to spring up almost daily. Due to the mechanics of gathering data and printing, some information may be several months out of date by the time the book reaches its reader. However, the basic information is stable.

Despite valiant efforts by publishers, it's impossible for any one directory to list every campground in the country. As a rule, if a camping area is missing, it's the owner's fault, not the publisher's. Even the giant among campground guides—Woodall's[4]—is not complete, although it is the size of the Manhattan telephone directory. During the past twenty years, there have been close to a hundred directories published. Few of them have survived, mostly due to the duplication of effort. While the leader, Woodall's, is a nationwide effort, there are also several good regional guide books to campgrounds.

[2] See the Appendix.
[3] See the Appendix.

[4] See the Appendix.

Attractive seaside campsites are sometimes difficult to find, but pretrip investigation helps to locate them. COLEMAN COMPANY

When shopping for such a guide, be sure it includes pertinent information, not mere generalities. It should include the campground's name; its location in relation to nearby towns and/or highways; tent and/or trailer facilities; phone number; post office address; availability of water, electricity, and firewood; type of sanitary facilities; proximity to stores and supplies; whether or not pets are permitted; presence of recreation buildings and/or programs, swimming, fishing, boating, hiking, mountain climbing, and rock hounding, plus nearby tourist attractions.

A campground's listing in a directory is not necessarily a recommendation of quality. Some gamble is involved in choosing a campground through one of these books. It's impossible, of course, for any publisher to inspect every facility listed in his book. It's to the credit of several directory publishers that they will withdraw the listing of a campground upon receipt of a legitimate and documented complaint.

CAMPGROUND OWNERS' ASSOCIATIONS

These consist of privately operated campgrounds, usually banded together for promotional purposes, lobbying, or direct mutual assistance. Part of the promotional efforts usually include the issuing of some sort of campground listing, sometimes in conjunction with state promotional bureaus. Listings in such literature are usually more detailed than that found in commercial directories, and though one might believe that glowing adjectives predominate, the fact is that most such associations maintain a strict code of honest and straightforward advertising. This code often includes minimum standards that must be maintained with regard to individual campsites, toilet and shower facilities, pricing, and facilities in general. In the Appendix you'll find a list of such campground owners' associations from whom you can obtain free literature.

While most federal and state areas will not accept advance reservations for a campsite, nearly all private campgrounds are anxious for this type of business and usually require only a small deposit—possibly $5 per week—to hold a site. This helps guarantee maximum occupancy for the area operator, but better still, it assures the camper of a site upon arrival. If you plan to remain in one campground for some time, such a reservation is almost a necessity, since the better campgrounds fill July and August bookings long before the season opens. If one or more areas is within reasonable driving distance, take a weekend or two for "shopping" prior to your vacation. Most campground operators welcome preseason visits and will accept a small deposit to hold a site. In all fairness to the owner, however, don't judge a campground by its appearance in April if it's not scheduled to open until June. Campgrounds are not at their best during preseason preparations, and you may find toilet buildings untidy (but about to be painted); tree limbs scattered about (but about to be cut into campers' firewood); roads muddy or rough from the spring thaw (but about to be scraped and smoothed).

CAMPING CLUBS AND ASSOCIATIONS

Only a small percentage of America's campers are members of clubs or associations devoted to the sport, but those who are members can obtain invaluable information from fellow club members or from the headquarters offices of larger groups. The information obtainable here is objective and accurate, since it is often first-hand—on a person-to-person basis. "Off the cuff" responses to queries will usually call a spade a spade. If the mosquitoes at Deep Gully Campground are big enough to carry away small children, you'll be told so, and if the toilet facilities at Puff Adder Camping Area are unkempt you'll be enlightened to that effect. Campers are quick to report to their clubs or associations shortcomings they've discovered in camping areas, and these reports get passed on to other members. At the same time, of course, the praises of popular and well-operated areas are spread rapidly. While few clubs or associations can actually plan trips for you, officers or office staff members will gladly answer specific questions. Chapter 21 describes some of the activities of various regional and national family-camping organizations.

TRAVEL PLANNING

If your objective is eating up the map with a stop at a different camping area each night, advance reservations may not be practical. A delay en route, an unexpected side trip, a laundromat stop, car trouble—any of these can throw a schedule out of kilter. On this type of trip, rely on a campground directory for locating each night's stopover area. A phone call during the afternoon will usually convince a private campground operator to hold a site for you until about six o'clock. If you can't make such an arrangement, have one or two alternate campgrounds picked out in case your first choice is brimming over with campers. In the case of state or federal campgrounds to which a phone call will probably be fruitless, bear in mind that popular areas start to fill by midafternoon, and overflow may jam even the second-rate parks. Plan to arrive no later than four o'clock, earlier if possible. Once you've located a suitable overnight spot, don't "go for broke," gambling that there'll be a better site a few miles down the road. You may end up sleeping in a motel, one of the venial sins of camping.

My heart always goes out to families who return from a "camping" trip to report, "We covered 8,971 miles in 19 days!" If the aim of a trip is simply to roll up mileage, you can probably allot a daily average of 450 to 500 miles along expressways, but, for all the pleasure and relaxation such travel affords, a camper might just as well go out to the local fairgrounds and drive 'round and 'round the track until the mileage goal is attained. A more reasonable daily mileage—say, 250 to 300 miles—will allow time for picnic stops, sightseeing, laundry stops, shopping, and early arrival at campgrounds. Also, you won't need a few extra days off the job during which to recover from your "vacation."

CAMPING TRIP COSTS

Few of us have unlimited budgets for camping or, as a matter of fact, for anything else. Estimating costs in advance is a vital part of planning and can be fairly accurate, providing, of course, that you stick to the budget. Particularly if there are children, this may prove futile. Parents on vacation are especially susceptible to pleas for extra ice cream stops or to the plaintive suggestion from a twelve-year-old boy, "Let's hire a boat, Dad, 'n' go fishin', just for one day, huh?" I'm not suggesting that a camping family mortgage its furniture to the Ever-Loving Finance Company, but if it's at all possible, include a few dollars to be squandered for sheer fun. Remember that car camping dif-

fers from wilderness camping. In the deep woods the simple pleasures of nature are free and priceless, but while traveling from campground to campground along our highways you'll encounter numberless attractions—zoos, museums, tramways, souvenir stands, and fairyland villages of all sorts—many of which are worthwhile seeing but which call for small cash expenditures.

Fortunate is the family planning to camp in or close to a wilderness area, especially if one or both of the parents has some knowledge and appreciation of nature. Passing this love on to their children is an adventure for both—examining a beaver house, watching sun dews devour tiny insects, searching out hidden partridge berries, learning to tell a white oak from a black—all of these can be fascinating entertainment and education even if the family's cash assets are all tied up in this week's grocery supply. A camping trip of this type may cost little more than staying home, the only "extras" being gasoline for the car and campsite fees.

In aligning your budget, there are certain "fixed" costs: car operation, food, campsite fees, and miscellaneous necessities such as fuel for the campstove and lantern, mantles, insect repellent, and laundry.

Then there are the "extras," without which you could very well vacation if need be, but since a holiday is supposed to be fun, you'll want to budget money for such things as boat rental and fishing licenses, souvenirs, postcards, film, and perhaps a dinner out and an evening at a summer theater.

What I'm tactfully trying to say is that only you can figure the price of your camping vacation. A family's spending habits at home tend to carry over—in fact, may even expand—during vacation trips. Spending comes easy to some and, if the financial means justify this, there's no reason for not enjoying some degree of affluence even while camping.

Chapter 17

WHERE TO CAMP

NATIONAL PARKS

The U.S. national parks, 38 of them totaling more than 14 million acres, are in effect great outdoor museums established by Congress to preserve areas of unusual natural beauty "in such a manner and by such means as will leave them unimpaired for the enjoyment of future generations." Under the jurisdiction of the National Park Service within the Department of the Interior, they are protected against industrial encroachment or business development—except by a rare act of Congress.

Because of their great beauty, usually excellent facilities, and in many instances fame, national parks bear the brunt of the annual camping crunch. Few of their campgrounds operate below capacity during the peak season. The National Park Service long ago recognized that it can never meet the peak-season demand for campsites, and has now put the brakes on campground expansion. It is not likely that a significant number of campsites will be added. Campgrounds mean roads, sewage disposal systems, rubbish handling, and, of course, concentrations of people, all detrimental to the natural beauty of the parks. Not only is campground expansion unlikely, but we may also see strict use limitations on facilities that already exist. A 1973 high-level study report urged the banning of recreational vehicles, with tents only to be permitted. This brought protests of "discrimination" from the Recreational Vehicle Institute, but don't be surprised if such a regulation is one day implemented, at least partially or regionally.

The National Park Service encourages campers to use private campgrounds that have appeared in recent years along the outside perimeter of the parks or near their entrances. Rather than forgoing a national park vacation when campgrounds are full, you can then at least enjoy the parks as day-use areas.

During the summers of 1973 and 1974, the National Park Service experimented with a nationwide system of campsite reservations. However, at this writing, announcement has been made that the reservation system is being abandoned, at least temporarily.

Early in 1933 I pitched my tent on a bluff overlooking a New Hampshire pond, where I stayed until well into October. I paid no campsite fee. There was no campsite, in fact. I carved one out of the shoreline woods. To this day, I don't know on whose land I squatted! Today I would be arrested for trespassing. Times change. Free and easy, unrestricted camping went out with the portholes on Buick mudguards. Get there early, or be prepared to stand in line during the busy season.

The National Park Service annually issues a booklet describing the areas under its jurisdiction. Details include acreage, location, outstanding characteristics, and postal address of the local headquarters from whom you can obtain more detailed information, such as a folder describing the specific park. The booklet is sold by the U. S. Government Printing Office.[1] The current issue comprises 192 pages and costs $.75, but this may vary from year to year.

Don't overlook the tremendous variety of attractions other than campgrounds administered by the National Park Service: battlefields, cemeteries, historic sites, lakeshores, memorials, military parks, monuments, parkways, seashores, and, among many others, the White House grounds. In short, the National Park Service operates the country's greatest tourist attractions. And I've never had an unpleasant visit in any of them.

NATIONAL FORESTS

These are the most misunderstood of all federal holdings, much of the confusion due to inaccurate press comments. One metropolitan daily recently stated on its editorial page: "Why bother with national forests if we allow them to cut down the trees?" This probably brought cheers from umpteen *nouveau* ecologists who think that trees live forever, but it was a journalistic blooper.

National forests are administered by the U. S. Forest Service, a part of the Department of Agriculture. This should be a tipoff. "Agriculture" implies crops. Trees are a crop. However, national forests have four major functions specified by law: (1) timber improvement and production, including the cutting and selling of logs; (2) watershed improvement and protection; (3) wildlife management, including hunting under state regulations; and (4) recreation.

The last time I counted, there were 153 national forests comprising 187 million acres. Recreation takes on many forms. Land is leased for ski resorts; trail bike and snowmobile trails are maintained; hiking trails crisscross the forests. Ski touring is on the increase, along with fishing, canoeing, hunting, and mountain climbing. Day-use areas are numerous, providing swimming, picnicking, and roadside rest stops, plus scenic overlooks or historical sites.

As for campsites, I doubt if the Forest Service knows exactly how many it has. I recall the figure: 30,000, but it's probably many more than that. Campgrounds range from relatively large facilities with flush toilets and electric lights

to primitive, bush-country clearings with nothing more than a crude stone fireplace. Don't look for hookups or a central TV antenna!

It would be impractical for the Forest Service to issue a one-volume directory of all of its campsites. The service is divided into regions: Northern, Rocky Mountain, Southwestern, California, Pacific Northwest, Southern, Eastern, and Alaska. Within each of these, regional campground directories are issued, most of them covering only one or two states, with some exceptions, notably the Eastern Region, which covers the area from Wisconsin to Maine and West Virginia northward.

The best source of information is not Washington, but any one of the 21 field offices listed in the *Forest Service Organizational Directory*, available from the U. S. Government Printing Office. The current copy costs $.60. This lists all field offices, ranger stations, and other installations, including the names, postal addresses, and telephone numbers of administrative officials. You'll learn much more about a specific national forest from the man who runs it than from his boss in Washington! You can, of course, obtain general information here, along with a listing of the regional offices.[2]

BUREAU OF LAND MANAGEMENT

An agency of the Department of the Interior, this bureau manages some 475 million acres in the public domain that have not been allocated to national parks, forests, or to other specific uses. These holdings are in the West and in Alaska. On these lands you'll encounter logging, cattle grazing, mining, and other industrial or commercial operations, plus camping!

Most BLM campgrounds are small and relatively primitive in country that ranges from arid to snow-covered. Campsites are generally of the get-away-from-it-all type, but there's no guarantee that you'll be alone. But such facilities often give you access to the backcountry, even though you may have to open and close a few gates and negotiate some rough roads. You may have to cross private land to reach some areas, for which you'll need permission or for which you may even have to pay a toll!

Don't conclude that the BLM has 475 million

[1] See the Appendix.

[2] See the Appendix.

When the crowds thin out in state parks, interesting off-season visitors join campers, in this case at Stephen Foster State Park in Georgia. GEORGIA DEPT. OF INDUSTRY AND TRADE

acres of glorious camping country. Some holdings are, frankly, junk land of little value even in today's inflated market. But, on the other hand, there are also numerous, vast sections of great beauty and outdoor appeal.

The BLM maintains campsites in Alaska, Arizona, California, Colorado, Idaho, Montana, Nevada, New Mexico, Oregon (which has the greatest number), South Dakota (the fewest), Utah, and Wyoming.

The Bureau issues superb descriptive folders and maps on a regional or state basis, these available from field offices.[3]

BUREAU OF RECLAMATION

Few Easterners know about this agency within the Department of the Interior. Its prime function under the 1902 National Reclamation Act is to construct and maintain dams, reservoirs, and canals for flood control and the irrigation of some 8 million acres in 17 western states. The Bureau also furnishes water to municipalities and hydroelectric plants. Offshoots of these projects, of course, are large manmade lakes along whose shores are more than 450 campgrounds providing close to 20,000 tent and recreational vehicle spaces. Some of these camping areas are operated by the Bureau, but most of them have been turned over to the Forest Service, the National Park Service, the Bureau of Sport Fisheries and Wildlife, various state fish and game departments, and local park, recreation, and water district agencies.

However, obtaining information is not as complex as it appears. The Bureau issues an excellent pamphlet briefly describing each campground, its facilities, location, administering agency, and its address.[4]

[3] See the Appendix.

[4] See the Appendix.

Bureau of Reclamation campgrounds are located on lakeshores in Arizona, California, Nevada, Utah, Colorado, New Mexico, Idaho, Wyoming, Kansas, Montana, Nebraska, North Dakota, Oklahoma, Oregon, South Dakota, Texas, and Washington.

BUREAU OF INDIAN AFFAIRS

The Bureau itself (another Department of the Interior agency) operates no campgrounds but encourages various tribes to bid actively for tourist business, including the operation of campgrounds. As a result, many tribes in the West, Southeast, and Upper Midwest share their lands with campers. Their campsites range from crudely primitive to modern, some of the latter supplying electric outlets, showers, phones, hookups, snack bars, and coin laundries. These campgrounds are owned and operated by the Indians, all profits accruing to the tribe. They are not, in any sense, government camping areas.

In addition to camping, many reservations offer hunting, fishing, boating, and swimming privileges at moderate fees. Some of the promotionally minded tribes conduct festivals and ceremonials for the benefit of visitors.

Despite the militancy detailed on TV newscasts (Wounded Knee in 1973, for example), Indians are gentle people and gracious hosts, but you will be required to conform to reservation regulations. Photograph ceremonials only by permission or when these are performed strictly for tourist entertainment. Respect certain sacred areas or symbols. Do not remove any artifacts (also against federal law!) or deface ruins.

This book is no place for a social commentary on our treatment of the Indians, but if you want to know more about them, there are several good works.[5]

You'll find Indian campgrounds in Arizona, California, Colorado, Florida, Michigan, Min-

nesota, Montana, Nebraska, New Mexico, North Carolina, North Dakota, Oklahoma, Oregon, South Dakota, Utah, Washington, and Wisconsin.

The Bureau of Indian Affairs[6] publishes a booklet detailing at some length Indian-operated campgrounds. Included are the mailing addresses of the various Indian agencies involved.

U. S. ARMY CORPS OF ENGINEERS

It's difficult for me to generate kindly thoughts about this agency, a subdivision of the Pentagon. According to its slide-rule generals, God was not fully competent at the time of our creation. He forgot to build any dams. The engineers have been correcting this shortcoming ever since they ran out of forts to build in Indian country. Some of our finest free-flowing rivers have been bottled up in concrete, and more are scheduled for imprisonment.

However, some good comes of this Tinker-Toy idiocy. Dams create lakes. And campers like lakeshores. By my last count some 31,402 campsites were available along the shoreline of impoundments in 30 states.

These are usually large-scale recreation areas offering not only camping but also water skiing, power boating, boat rentals, launching ramps, guest cabins, organized camps, and marinas. If you like intensive activity and lots of people, look into these campsites.

The Corps of Engineers issues a pamphlet describing the location of its facilities and the extent of their development.[7]

TENNESSEE VALLEY AUTHORITY (TVA)

This system parallels that of the Army Corps of Engineers except that it is confined to the Tennessee River watershed in Alabama, Georgia, Kentucky, Mississippi, North Carolina, Tennessee, and Virginia. It consists of a series of dams that create 36 reservoirs with interconnecting improved riverways, canals, and boat locks.

Along the shores are no fewer than 14 state parks, and at some points, national park and

[5] U. S. Department of Commerce, *Federal and State Indian Reservations* (Washington, D.C.: U. S. Government Printing Office, 1971); Judith C. Ullom, *Folklore of the North American Indians* (Washington, D.C.: U. S. Government Printing Office, 1969); Ralph K. Andrist, *The Long Death* (New York: Macmillan, 1964); Dee Brown, *Bury My Heart at Wounded Knee* (New York: Holt, Rinehart & Winston, 1970).

[6] See the Appendix.
[7] See the Appendix.

forest lands abut the waterways. There are also more than 75 public parks operated by county and municipal agencies. Maps and charts of the waterways are available.[8]

In addition, there is the famed Land Between the Lakes,[9] a 40-mile strip of land between Kentucky and Barkley lakes, an all-'round recreation area developed by the TVA. Camping is strongly accented. While the original TVA function was to provide electricity (it operates numerous hydro- and steam-generating electric plants), the project now provides almost unlimited recreation of all types associated with camping and the outdoors in general. The TVA issues a complete directory and map of the giant facility.[10]

BUREAU OF SPORT FISHERIES AND WILDLIFE

A part of the Department of the Interior, this agency operates more than 300 wildlife refuges totaling close to 30 million acres in every state except New Hampshire, Rhode Island, Connecticut, and West Virginia, although since this writing, it's possible that areas have been established in one or more of these states. Few realize that fishing and hunting are permitted on certain refuges under special regulations and only for specific species. But the prime objective is the protection and propagation of all forms of wildlife; visitors are always welcome, but only to the extent that they do not interfere with wildlife management. Many refuges operate interpretive centers where the work is explained, but it is the natural environment, zealously protected against encroachment by man, that is fascinating. These are essentially pockets of true wilderness.

Camping is permitted on a few wildlife refuges, but bear in mind that recreation is secondary. There are few, if any, "posh" campgrounds, only simple facilities for those who appreciate a close-up of nature. The Bureau issues literature available either from Washington or from its field offices.[11]

[8] Write: TVA Maps, Knoxville, Tennessee 37902 or Chattanooga, Tennessee 37401.
[9] Write: Land Between the Lakes, TVA, Golden Pond, Kentucky 42231.
[10] See the Appendix.
[11] See the Appendix.

THE GOLDEN EAGLE PASSPORT

Originated as part of the Land and Water Conservation Fund Act passed by Congress in 1964, the first Golden Eagle Passport was a car sticker, costing $7.00 annually, that admitted any noncommercial vehicle and its occupants to most federal recreation areas where an entry fee existed. It was, and still is, misunderstood. It did *not* provide for free use of facilities, only free entry.

Also, the Act had to be renewed by Congress every year, which it failed to do several times. The program lapsed, and federal park and forest officials reinstituted their own charge systems. Confusion resulted, especially when the Congress restored the program in midseason!

Finally, in 1972, Congress made the Golden Eagle Passport a permanent institution. The fee went to $10, but it still covered only the entry into an area. Charges for camping, boat launching, etc., where these existed, were continued, even to holders of the passport.

In addition, Congress created the Golden Age Passport, a free-entry permit for those over 65. It was made available at no charge through post offices. It also provided a 50 per cent discount from camping fees and other use charges.

Then, in 1973, Congress passed and President Nixon signed an amendment to the Land and Water Conservation Fund Act that eliminated all charges for the use of facilities that did not include all of the following: flush toilets, showers, access and circulatory roads, sanitary disposal systems, visitor protection patrols, designated tent and trailer sites, refuse containers, and potable water.

These stiff requirements eliminated charges at thousands of national forest and park campgrounds. The Golden Eagle and Golden Age passports are still in effect. But where "golden agers" used to camp at a 50 per cent discount, they now camp free. If they stop at highly developed areas, the 50 per cent discount still applies. As for the Golden Eagle Passport, it still does away with daily entry fees where such fees are still charged.

It's all very confusing! And it's unrealistic to believe that the federal government can go on providing free camping and other recreation in the face of ever-increasing demand.

Indirectly, too, towns that have lands within

A folding tent trailer can be maneuvered into a remote campsite. The trick is to find such a site. NIMROD

national forest boundaries receive 25 per cent of the forest's revenue to use for schools and roads. They will now lose the recreation portion of these allotments.

But I'm sure that the continuing story of the Golden Eagle Passport is not ended. The next episode will surely be as confusing![12]

STATE PARKS

The variety of layout, terrain, climate, and sports available in state parks brings one to the conclusion that there is no "typical" state campground. Generally speaking, however, in the developed parks you'll find paved roads, flush toilets, possibly hot showers, a supervised swimming area, moderately well-spaced campsites, ample firewood (for which there may

[12] Congress reinstated fees in federal areas in 1974, thus making the Golden Eagle and the Golden Age passports worthwhile. However, these are no longer handled by post offices and must be obtained from offices at any federal recreation area.

be a small charge), and a setting of scenic beauty or historical significance. You'll probably be charged fees comparable to those in privately operated, basic-facility campgrounds.

Until recent years, state park campgrounds were generally on the primitive side. But with the increase in the number of self-contained recreational vehicles, most new parks offer some type of hookups and/or a sanitary disposal station. Some older parks have added the latter.

State parks are likely to be crowded during July and August, and there may be a waiting line. In a few states, reservations may be made. As a rule, the length of stay is limited to about two weeks.

Of course, there are more primitive state parks, with facilities limited to a rustic table, fireplace, spring, and a one-seat structure. On the other hand, more elaborate areas may offer Adirondack lean-to shelters for rent, possibly even cabins. Some maintain interpretive programs, with guided tours and evening lectures by naturalists. There may be nature trails, riding paths with horses for hire, boat launching and docking facilities, a supply store, museum, or zoo.

In order to discover your own favorite, you have only to embark upon a tour of those state parks within vacation-time driving distance of home, following a winter's reading of park folders.

All states[13] issue these, but due to the increasing camper crunch and growing complaints by residents that they are being crowded (by nonresidents) out of parks that they (the residents) pay for, many states have toned down their promotional efforts. Some states set aside portions of campgrounds for resident use only, and it's only a matter of time before entire campgrounds are reserved for residents. So if you're planning a state park trip, it's wise to inquire in advance about the availability of campsites, and where possible, to make a reservation.

STATE FORESTS

In many states—Massachusetts, for example—state forests and parks are indistinguishable, so far as the general public is concerned. While the original purpose of state forests was the conservation and improvement of timberlands and the protection of watersheds, recreation has become an important by-product. New Jersey, Wisconsin, and Connecticut have developed state forest campgrounds, for example, that compare favorably with the better campgrounds in many state parks.

State-operated conservation areas and wildlife refuges, too, are often open to camping, although facilities are likely to be primitive or even nonexistent. Such areas make it possible for campers to experience semiwilderness camping close to home.

COUNTY AND MUNICIPAL PARKS

County parks are generally well known only within a relatively small area. Few attain any regional popularity. One exception is the Belknap-Gunstock Recreation Area near Laconia, New Hampshire, operated by Belknap County.

[13] See the Appendix.

This is a highly developed 500-site campground with all the comforts and delights, including a 1½-mile chair lift. Undoubtedly there are other fine county parks, but they are not well known.

During the twenties and thirties, municipal park campgrounds were common, but the Depression converted many to hangouts for drifters, resulting in the closing of most of the campgrounds. There is some trend back to municipal parks today, however. The city of Burlington, Vermont, operates an outstanding park with campground on the shores of Lake Champlain.

The crying need currently is for camping and recreational vehicle parks close to major cities. Motels and glorified hot-dog stands blight their outskirts, but if a camper wants to park his rig while visiting in town, he has to commute from the boondocks. By way of contrast, several of Europe's major cities have tenting and trailer areas within their city limits—apparently aware that campers, too, enjoy visits to museums, plays, concerts, and shopping centers.

PRIVATE CAMPGROUNDS

Private campgrounds are "private" only in the sense that they are owned by individuals or privately controlled firms. They are the camping counterpart of hotels and motels—open to the public. They run the gamut from primitive to posh and, although few of them are in settings comparable to Yosemite, Yellowstone, or Acadia, many are in attractive, wooded, lakeside, or streamside locations. No longer is an abandoned pasture or other submarginal land suitable for camping. Many a handsome pine grove heretofore nurtured for timber harvesting has been converted into a camping area for profit. Campers who prefer simple facilities, however, will generally find few private areas without "lace curtain" frills. A few, of course, provide "camping in the rough" facilities, but they are a minority.

Increasingly, private family campgrounds are becoming plush tent and trailer resorts, boasting such luxuries as flush toilets; hot showers; automatic washers and driers; electricity at individual sites; sewer and water hookups; swimming pools; playgrounds; recreation buildings; and entertainment, which may range from square dancing to fish fries. And already existing in some areas (and soon to come in others) are such luxuries as phone and TV plug-ins, attendants who will park your rig, "site service" (like room service in a hotel!) for snacks or ice cubes, baby sitters, putting greens, tennis courts, marinas, full-fledged restaurants, and inns where campers' guests may stay. For the busy executive roughing it for a few days, you might also look for a helicopter pad and a direct stock market wire. Several motel chains are developing recreational vehicle facilities so that travelers can utilize both types of facilities.

Private campgrounds generally cater to recreational vehicle users or to families with little or no camping experience, and families with young children to whom a wilderness trip could be hazardous. It's not unreasonable for a young mother with two or three children under six to prefer an area that offers ample hot water and a well-lighted comfort station with flush toilets. Families with teen-agers, too, find such campgrounds a blessing because of activities slanted to these young people. An old woodsman friend of mine expressed recently that "them fancy campgrounds is fine—keeps city folks outa my fishing holes." His attitude may not be in the true spirit of sharing our outdoor heritage, but he has a valid point.

Camping fees in private areas are invariably higher than in public campgrounds for the simple reason that they are built with private funds and operated for profit, being simply another facet of the resort business. While it may nonplus the wilderness camper, the overwhelming majority of family campers prefer the comforts-of-home luxuries in private areas and are willing to pay the larger fees. Up to a point, of course! One overrated and highly touted area an hour's drive from my home upped its lakeshore site fees to $12 per day. It filed for bankruptcy shortly thereafter.

State associations of campground owners[14] have set up minimum standards that benefit campers. Some are strictly enforced, others are not. The result is that quality varies. Some should be closed down. But on the whole, private operators strive to provide a pleasurable experience. Most state associations issue a free directory of the membership.

The big advantage of using private campgrounds, of course, is that you can reserve a site in advance and remain as long as you like. Few public areas accept reservations, and nearly all limit the length of stay during the busy season.

Another concept of private campgrounds is the condominium. Here you *buy* a campsite, to use as much or as little as you like. When not in use, the management will rent it for you in some cases. Condominium campsites are usually in luxurious campgrounds; hence they're expensive—some as high as $10,000!

A private camp lot may be the answer for some families. This can be a piece of real estate, one acre or fifty, of rural land, which you might buy with eye to erecting a cabin later. In the meantime, you can camp on it. There's never a "No Vacancy" sign!

FRANCHISED CAMPGROUNDS

Most of these are locally owned and operated, built according to a standard design supplied by the franchise company, which also does national advertising, provides a directory,[15] and assists in other ways to promote the chain. The owner pays the franchise company a flat fee initially, then an annual commission. Quality among these varies. Some franchisers inspect member campgrounds to see that standards are maintained. Others are simply promotional agencies.

One advantage of staying at franchised campgrounds is the national reservation system some maintain, much like that of the major motel and hotel chains.

Generally, franchised campgrounds are quite good. If you find one that is not, contact the parent company, specifying your complaint clearly. The chances are that action will be taken.

TIMBERLAND COMPANY AREAS

It wasn't too many years ago that many timberland owners closed their privately built and maintained roads to the public—and particularly to campers. Many have since had a public relations change of heart and now welcome campers, even to the extent of providing camping areas. Some timberland still remains closed to

[14] See the Appendix.

[15] See the Appendix.

Camping at Whycocomagh, in the interior of Cape Breton Island. CANADIAN GOVERN-
MENT TRAVEL BUREAU

campers—dangerous slash areas and regions
along woods roads where logging trucks are a
hazard to cars—but apart from these sections,
millions of acres have been made accessible.
This is not a localized phenomenon but a coun-
trywide trend among the nation's largest land-
holders, one that has resulted in the "Welcome"
sign being hung out in virtually every commercial forest in the nation. Close to one hundred thousand miles of company roads are open
to the public, giving access to camping, hunting,
fishing, winter sports, hiking, boating, and other
forms of outdoor recreation. Some companies
charge small fees.

I'm surprised that higher fees (and more of
them) are not charged. Major complaints of
the loggers concern the destruction of signs by
visitors, littering, theft of company property,
vandalism of buildings temporarily out of use,
destruction of gates, illegal cutting of Christmas
trees, and the ever-present bugaboo—starting
forest fires! Despite this, many companies main-

tain a recreational planner. Loggers deserve better treatment.

Information concerning individual timberland
companies is somewhat difficult to obtain due to
their great number, but helpful literature is
available from the American Forest Institute.[16]

CANADIAN NATIONAL PARKS

I've found campgrounds in Canada's national
parks to be superbly operated and usually in
beautifully scenic sections of the parks. High-
intensity areas are known as "serviced" campgrounds, which means they have permanent attendants and staff and provide such niceties
as electricity, hookups, interpretive programs,
showers, and patrols. "Semiserviced" areas have
fewer facilities, although your needs will be
amply fulfilled, including periodic visits by attendants. More remote campgrounds are rela-

[16] See the Appendix.

tively unimproved, with primitive (though safe) water supply from a brook or spring, and toilets of the outhouse type. Camping in other areas is not permitted.

National parks in the Far West—British Columbia and Alberta—boast some of the finest mountain scenery in the world, some capped by year-'round glaciers and snowfields. I recall climbing at 8,000 feet in July having left my camp that morning where the temperature was close to 70°! Banff and Jasper, of course, are the two famous parks, but there are others equally beautiful.

The "prairie" parks in eastern Alberta, Saskatchewan, and Manitoba may seem less attractive to a "woods camper," but their charm and beauty grow on you. These are not truly "prairie" parks, actually, being located in large "islands" of woodlands. Riding Mountain National Park in Manitoba is one of these.

The national parks of central Canada generally cluster about the Great Lakes and the St. Lawrence River. Those in the East—among them, Fundy National Park is close to being the perfect family recreation area in either the United States or Canada—are maritime associated. All are on or close to the sea.

PROVINCIAL PARKS

These are the Canadian counterparts of American state parks, fewer in number possibly but much larger in area. In fact, most south-of-the-border parks seem little more than woodlots when compared to the vastness of some of the provincial recreation regions.

One of the handsomest is Rushing River in Ontario. Mistassini and Chibougamau in Quebec are vast, much of them little more than raw wilderness, with Indians camped by the roadside in ever-present shear-rigged wall tents. Laurentide, also in Quebec, is beautifully mountainous, although high-tension power lines criss-

Beautifully wooded campsite in Fundy National Park, New Brunswick. CANADIAN GOVERNMENT TRAVEL BUREAU

crossing overhead along the main road somewhat mar the beauty.

It's impossible to detail even briefly all of
the outstanding provincial parks. I've cited these
few from personal experience only as examples
of the variety you'll find throughout Canada.
Contact the various provincial tourist agencies
for colorful literature.[17]

Border-crossing formalities have been minimized to the extent that they are little more
than cordial greetings at the boundary station.
However, a list of such items as cameras, outboard motors, binoculars, portable radios, and
similar equipment will expedite crossing into
Canada. Pistols and automatic rifles may not
be taken into Canada. For re-entering the United
States, birth certificates or naturalization certificates are helpful. Otherwise, you may have to
prove citizenship.

[17] See the Appendix.

MEXICO

Frankly, my personal knowledge of Mexico
is rather limited, although I've gotten to know
many Mexican people and like them tremen-
dously. My exposure to Mexico came when I
served with the U. S. Border Patrol at El Paso,
Texas, where, unfortunately, my contacts were
with the fringe ilk rather than with the average
Mexican family. During an occasional day off,
however, we crossed the Rio Grande and found
most Mexicans friendly, open-hearted, and re-
ceptive to helping a stranger in their midst.
Forget about the *bandidos* of the movies and
TV. If they exist, I never saw one—and remember, we were looking for them up and down the
Rio Grande! The typical American vision of a
Mexican is a horrendous distortion. My only re-
gret about my tour of duty on the southern
border is that I did not get to know more
Mexican people.

Double-checking the rig aboard a flatcar for a Mexican piggyback train ride. GIL ANDRES

Under way, campers in the rigs "let the engineer do the driving." GIL ANDRES

I'm not qualified to give you tips on camping in Mexico, but Dan Sanborn, of McAllen, Texas, is. He sells insurance to travelers headed into Mexico where American automobile policies are not valid. You need special coverage.

Whether you buy insurance from him or not, he'll send you a free trip-planning kit[18] that covers every aspect of auto travel in Mexico. Even before you leave, you can become a pretty fair authority simply by reading this material. It is highly detailed. Little is overlooked.

If you buy your insurance from him he'll supply you with maps and travel logs, mile-by-mile instructions, plus where-to-eat and where-to-stay information. He's not shy about rating campgrounds. Dan has offices at all major points of entry into Mexico.

It is not necessary that you buy your insurance from him. Several other excellent firms offer equally good coverage. I'm citing Sanborn's because I know of no one who has so thoroughly researched and experienced car travel in Mexico and who issues such detailed, step-by-step information.

A fascinating recreational vehicle possibility in Mexico is a railroad piggyback service. You can load your camper aboard a flatcar, to which it will be firmly secured. Then you can ride through unbelievably beautiful country while enjoying the comfort and convenience of your rig. Leave the driving to the engineer!

Gil Andres operates this service on the Ferrocarril al Pacifico out of El Paso.[19] You can't hire a single flatcar as part of a regular freight train, of course. The entire train is made of flatcars bearing recreational vehicles from all over the United States, as far as Mazatlan and back to El Paso.

Another possibility is a conducted tour or "caravan." Travel clubs sponsored by makers of various recreational vehicles operate these group tours. Most are accompanied by a doctor, a mechanic, and a Mexican insurance adjuster.

EUROPE, EASTERN AND WESTERN, AND THE REST OF THE WORLD

An excellent source of information on camping in Europe and many other parts of the globe is George S. Wells, a writer of many fine camping books and publisher of *Camping Guide* magazine.[20] Some years ago, George organized Camping Guide Tours, Inc,[21] which arranges group trips overseas (and to Alaska), combining air travel and equipment rental. Group rates keep costs down.

[18] See the Appendix.

[19] See the Appendix.
[20] See the Appendix.
[21] See the Appendix.

Complete camping and touring outfit available in Europe through planned group or individual tours. CONTINENTAL CAMPERS

The program is constantly being expanded and currently includes Western Europe, South America, Iceland, Greenland, Jamaica, Hawaii, Rhodesia, South Africa, Kenya, Japan, Australia, and New Zealand.

Other agencies conduct similar trips. You have only to contact a travel agent for suggestions and help. Travel agents charge nothing for their services; their incomes are derived from commissions on air fares, camper rentals, etc. They can help you join a group tour or plan an individualized trip for you.

Several agencies also arrange for recreational vehicle rentals in Europe.[22] You simply fly to a major European city, pick up the camper (they're usually fully equipped with all but food), and set out to see the Old World.

It is also possible to ship your recreational vehicle overseas via boat, picking it up at dockside. You can either "accompany" it on the boat or make a quick flight timed to meet the boat.

With the easing of the strain between the East and the West there's considerable interest in the Soviet Union by American sportsmen and campers. And the Soviets are eager to develop their tourist industry. Some small campgrounds exist, including one near Moscow designated primarily for foreigners. However, such facilities are very limited, few, and far apart. Mass camping, as we know it, is unknown. There is a camping movement but it is usually associated with mountain climbing, fishing, and in some instances with hunting. Outdoor recreation facilities exist, some quite extensive, but they are usually slanted toward such sports as skiing, swimming, gymnastics, basketball, hockey, all with overtones of competition.

Parks, as we know them, do not exist. All of the land is publicly owned, hence when a Soviet goes out into the country, he camps on "his" land. Not without restrictions, of course. Fire laws are enforced and indiscriminate cutting of trees is frowned upon, illegal in many parts.

There is, however, a move to assist people into enjoying the outdoors. During the winter of 1973–74, a three-man team made up of Bill Worff, a top official in the U. S. Forest Service, Bob Barbee, his counterpart in the National Park Service, and myself spent five weeks in the Soviet Union with the U. S. Information Service exhibit:

[22] See the Appendix.

You can ship your own rig overseas for a leisurely ship cruise and a continental tour.
ACL

Outdoor Recreation U.S.A. More than ten thousand persons per day crowded the showroom to view American outdoor gear. A total of some two million Soviet citizens visited the show to view our tents, canoes, fishing tackle, rifles and shotguns, skis, mountaineering gear—even a motor home!

During our stay, we were visited by five top officials from the Soviet Republic of Georgia, who flew some 300 miles to meet us. Their purpose? To learn about the American system of national parks and forests so that they might possibly set up a similar system with the accent on outdoor recreation!

Presently, family camping behind the iron curtain borders on pioneering. It *is* being developed. But for the time being, it's for the adventurous. If you're in that category and want to try it, you'll have to work through a travel agent who deals with Intourist, the official Soviet government tourist department. This is easy, since virtually all American travel agents who handle foreign flights can pave the way for you.

Chapter 18

MOTHER NATURE IS NO LADY

WEATHER

Professional outdoorsmen are rarely surprised by a "sudden storm," and a rapid temperature drop during the night seldom poses a problem. On the other hand, since most of us are encased in the protective walls of suburban or city environment and dependent upon the TV weatherman, we have lost the knack for anticipating Mother Nature's next move. Because "the stars were shining last night" we awaken in the morning surprised to hear raindrops dancing on the tent roof. We shiver in inadequate bedding during a "summer vacation" when the night temperature plummets to 35 degrees following a warm day. We wonder why the wind blows all day and into the night on one occasion, then drops at sunset on another. It's all very baffling.

No one can make accurate-to-the-minute predictions, that we know, but it *is* possible to anticipate many changes in weather, even lacking a radio, TV set, or barometer.

For many years, on our camping and canoe trips, we've applied weather rhymes to the natural signs we observe. One of these, while not infallible, is surprisingly reliable:

> When the wind is in the South,
> The rain is in its mouth.

This is the wind that may rise during the day and blow all night, often bringing rain within a few hours. The rainstorm accompanying a south wind is usually short-lived, but one borne on the wrath of a northeast blow may rage for several days, except on the west coast of Florida and on the continental west coast. On the other hand, winds from the north, west, and southwest are clearing winds, and the more northerly they are, the cooler the air they carry. Unlike a wind from the south, these usually drop at sunset, but don't be surprised to see them rise again come morning. A northwest blow, although clear, may last two to three days.

Even a windless day helps predict weather, and there's a rhyme to fit this case, too:

> A stormy day will betide,
> Sound traveling far and wide.

Sound travels "far and wide" on a quiet day, one usually completely without wind. Smoke hangs in low places, particularly at evening, and you can hear clearly the voices of campers across the lake. Sometimes, too, the leaves of hardwoods turn their undersides upward. Rain is on the way.

> Red sky at night, sailor's delight,
> Red sky at morning, sailors take warning

is another apt rhyme. If the sun rises as a glowing orange-red ball through a grayish haze, chances are you'll have rain before the day is out. If it *sets* in this manner, although the haze may not be as pronounced, fine weather will follow. Such a sunset during a heat wave means a continuation of the humidity and high temperatures. However, if the sun sets through a graying mass of thin clouds—even though it is a glowing ball of red—look for rain if the western sky is streaked with yellow or green tinges. This also indicates high winds on the way.

A sundog or halo around the sun, caused by sunlight filtering through ice particles at high altitudes, is another indication of rain. Similarly, a ring around the moon often portends wet weather. The popular belief that "the bigger the ring, the nearer the wet" is unreliable, nor can you rely on the saying that the number of stars within the ring is equal to the number of days before the rain. That would be convenient, though.

A quarter moon with the "horns" pointing downward is not necessarily a "wet moon," nor do the "horns" pointing upward always indicate clear weather. However, the moon does help to the extent that when the points stand out sharply in the night sky, high winds will follow. If hazy, calm weather is due. A brilliantly white moon forecasts clear days to follow, whereas a tinge of yellow or orange on its surface is an indication of rain approaching. This appraisal should be made when the moon is well up into its zenith, however. Seen through the earth's atmosphere when it first rises, it almost always appears yellowish.

Certain cloud formations foretell weather, and these have produced the old-time sailor's rhyme:

Mackerel sky and mare's tails
Make tall ships carry low sails.

Mackerel clouds are cirrocumulus, in a pattern that resembles mackerel scales. Mare's tails are cirrus clouds—thin, wispy curls that fly at extreme speeds, sometimes more than 200 miles per hour, at high altitudes. When mare's tails form a filmy overcast above a widespread area of mackerel sky, rain is on the way within a day or two. Sometimes this cloud combination appears for just a few minutes, but an experienced outdoorsman won't miss it.

Those evenly spaced "puffball" clouds with rounded edges, so often seen in the summer sky, are cumulus formations. They indicate good weather. However, when these begin to bunch together and their edges grow ragged, "towers" or "parapets" will form atop them. These then proceed to develop into stratocumulus, which will turn dark and lower rapidly in preparation for an imminent rain. These clouds lose no time in wetting down the earth.

Predicting a thunderstorm isn't a particularly difficult feat. Nearly everyone is familiar with the towering thunderheads, and as the storm approaches, there's the rumble of thunder and the flash of lightning. However, few know that only a thunderstorm coming from the west or northwest will strike you with the full brunt of its force. You can, in fact, draw an imaginary east-west line through your campsite to help you appraise the possibilities of an approaching thunderstorm. The centers of storms to the east have already passed you. These won't "turn around and come back," as is sometimes believed. The center of a thunderstorm visible to the south of your imaginary line will also miss you, although its northern fringes may make a swipe at you, possibly with considerable force. interim. When flashes of lightning begin to approaching from the west along this imaginary line, or from a position slightly north of the line, has mayhem in its eye aimed directly at you.

Don't rely on winds to keep a thunderstorm at bay. Very often I've seen vicious storms bear down from the northwest while a firm breeze from the southwest blew on the earth's surface. This contrary wind often continues until within a few moments of the storm's striking. Usually there are a few minutes of dead calm in the interim. When flashes of lightning begin to appear, you can estimate the distance to the storm by counting the seconds between the time you see a flash and the moment you hear the thunder. The sound of thunder travels at 1,100 feet per second, so that it takes the thunder's rumbling about 5 seconds to travel 1 mile. Divide your count by 5 and you have the number of miles.

One of the safest places during a thunderstorm is in a recreational vehicle or in an automobile. The metal body is a protective casing, and the tires insulate you against the sky/earth charge. The most dangerous situation arises when you cause yourself to become the most prominent object on the landscape, or when you are close to one. Stand alone in an open field, or under a tree in a clearing, and you become a natural, probable target. This explains the frequent deaths by lightning on golf courses. Standing in a small cave may also be hazardous. A ground charge may use your body as a conductor from ceiling to floor, or vice versa. A mountainside gully, one angling upward steeply, is often a natural channel for lightning.

There are few experts on the subject of lightning, and even these often disagree. The behavior of lightning is frequently unexplainable. My grandfather, a logger in Wisconsin, once led a pair of horses into the barn, seeking to escape a thunderstorm. As he walked between the horses, lightning hit, killing both animals. He escaped with bruises.

Don't use electrical outlets in campground comfort stations during a storm; stay away from metal pipes and wire fences, and should you visit a forest fire lookout tower, never remain in one during a storm. A tower that I manned during my early days in the woods had had two persons killed in it!

Lightning kills about six hundred persons annually in the United States. Automobiles kill a greater number every week. You're safer on a campground than on the expressway, but only if you follow the simple, common-sense rules I've cited.

Fog is usually associated with sea stories and murder mysteries, but it also has its place as a weather sign. It too has a rhyme:

> Evening fog will not burn soon,
> Morning fog will burn 'fore noon.

If you awaken in camp to find that you can't see the length of the picnic table through the fog, rest assured that a good day is in store for you. The fog will "burn off 'fore noon." However, if the fog rolls in during the late afternoon or evening, it will be with you all night, though not necessarily followed by rain.

One of the easiest of weather signs to recognize, and one of the most reliable, is dew—or a lack of it. This sign rates three rhymes:

> When the grass is dry at morning light,
> Look for rain before the night.

> When the grass is dry at night,
> Look for rain before the light.

> When the dew is on the grass,
> Rain will not come to pass.

Not all weather omens rhyme, of course. If someone could write a couplet rhyming "smell" and "skunk," it might prove to be a major contribution to amateur weather predicting. Smells are more pronounced just before a storm. Low pressure moving in makes the odors of swamps, cooking, and skunks more perceptible. Too, don't laugh at a friend who proclaims: "It's going to rain. My corn hurts." Arthritis, old wounds, bunions, and corns react to this same low pressure, thus "predicting" rain.

There are innumerable signs not covered by weather ditties, some fairly accurate, others little more than superstitions or old wives' tales. Sea gulls, for example, remain close to shore—the sign of coming rain according to many seaside residents. Woodsmen will vouch for a coming storm when deer leave high ground and seek the shelter of thick growth in the lowlands. Crows fly crazily, darting erratically. The rain crow, really a yellow- or black-billed cuckoo, emits its throaty croak. Swallows fly low over the water. Cows all lie down, facing in one direction. And, probably the most unbelievable of all, bits of soot fall from the fireplace chimney. Too, there's the old saying: "Rain before seven, clear before eleven."

Though many of us would like to believe them, natural weather signs are not infallible, although many have an amazingly high batting average. However, like any thorough professional, a skilled outdoorsman, upon seeing one sign, searches for others to corroborate the first. If he finds two or more, then he usually makes his prediction with a surprising degree of accuracy.

POISONOUS PLANTS

Why is it that so many roadside "historical markers" are set in poison ivy beds? Eleanor and I, being history buffs, stopped our car in central Massachusetts one day last summer to inspect the site of a barracks that had housed Hessian soldiers during the American Revolution. We arrived only a moment too late to warn some nine tourists, apparently all from the same family, that they'd just been strolling leisurely through one of the lushest beds of poison ivy we had ever seen. It amazes me that so many persons with interests in the outdoors don't learn to recognize it. Everyone, of course, knows that "it's shiny and has three leaves." The fact is that while poison ivy does have groups of three leaves, they are not necessarily shiny. Frequently they are dull. They may be dark or light green, small and close to the ground, or large and growing almost a foot tall. Ivy creeps over stone walls, climbs trees, and is most commonly found along country roads where passing automobiles and road scrapers help to spread it mile after mile. This variety of color, form, and locale *is* baffling. However, there is

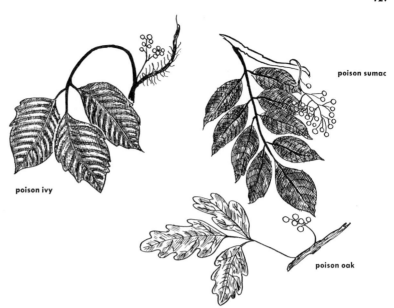

The common poisonous plants.

one unique characteristic about poison ivy that anyone can learn to recognize at a glance. This is seen in the stem of the leaf. The stem in the main leaf bisects it perfectly. The stem in each of the two side leaves is somewhat off center, so that the half of the leaf nearest the main leaf is smaller than the other half. It's that simple to recognize poison ivy.

An apparent "immunity" isn't to be trusted. During some forty years in the woods I've disregarded poison ivy, sometimes walking through it deliberately rather than detouring, especially when wearing my heavy "woods boots." And it never bothered me—until 1972, when I "caught it" from the knees down while clearing a new road around my barn where I ignored a luscious bed of those "three shiny leaves"! Eleanor, who also had never been infected, came down with the "itch" when she assisted with the project.

Some persons have a high degree of susceptibility to it, and they can acquire a severe case simply by patting a dog that has walked among a few plants. Exposure to the poison can come about by changing a tire on a car that has been driven through the ivy, and some persons may be infected merely by walking through smoke from a fire whose fuel includes poison ivy.

Despite the standard jokes, ivy poisoning is not to be treated lightly. If you suspect infection, see a physician. He probably can't stop the itch completely, but he can help you avoid more severe reactions. Early symptoms are red,

itchy blotches on the skin. Blisters usually follow, and often severe swelling. I've seen cases where the victim's eyes were nearly shut by such swelling. The misery of poison ivy isn't to be taken lightly, and self-treatment of any but the lightest cases may result only in aggravating that misery.

The best precaution is to learn to recognize poison ivy (and that goes for poison sumac and poison oak, too). You'll find guidelines and illustrations in numerous books, but the best way is to inspect the plant in the field while accompanied by someone who knows!

WILD ANIMALS

With regard to these, family campers seem to fall into three catagories: (1) those with a deep-seated, genuine fear of all wild things; (2) those with no fear whatsoever of anything that walks, flies, swims, or creeps; and (3) the minority who understand and respect wildlife for exactly what it is—wild.

Deep-rooted, unreasoning fear is difficult to overcome, despite all sorts of reassurances. To a person convinced that a bear will attack on sight, that a cougar waits on a ledge along the trail, and that snakes lie in ambush behind every rock, camping out requires tremendous courage. Such persons need understanding, not the ridicule that is usually their lot.

On the other hand, a "fearless" camper who attempts to hand-feed or pet a so-called "tame" bear at a campground dump or by a park roadside is utterly stupid or suicidal! Even more incredible is the young couple whom my son watched trying to set their youngster astride a yearling bear for a photo! The she-bear was close by!

Since I spend much time in the woods where bear abound, I've encountered at least a dozen, at various distances ranging from a canoe-length confrontation up to a hundred feet or so. These were wild bear. In every single instance except one, the bear fled pell-mell! In the case of the exception, I deliberately provoked a she-bear (I was then a young, foolish guide) by approaching her cubs. I had to shoot her, something I've regretted ever since.

The most dangerous animal in the United States is the park bear turned scavenger. He has lost his natural fear of man, but not his ability to kill with one swift blow of a forepaw. Wild animals don't understand "giving" as humans do. It is their nature to "take." There is no "kindness," as we know it, in nature; only the availability of food or the lack of it. So when parents allow a child to feed a "cute" bear part of a hot dog, they risk the child's life. The bear recognizes the youngster only as another animal. That animal has a choice tidbit in its paw. So the bear will take it, either gently or with a swift, horrifying, maiming attack. There's no predicting which.

Another travesty of the wild is the "Bambi syndrome," the result of "outdoorsy" movies and TV dramas that attribute human characteristics to wild animals. Deer are beautiful, appealing animals, and they are easy to tame. But making a pet of a wild deer is a cruel hoax. A deer's normal diet includes grass, raspberry buds, even toadstools. But tourists persist in feeding them cookies, popcorn, candy bars, marshmallows, and other assorted junk on which kids live these days. Reverse the situation for a moment. What would you do if someone tried to feed your child a handful of grass? Or a few half-rotted beech nuts?

Hand-feeding and taming a deer dispels its fear of man. And this is where cruelty lies. The first deer to be shot on opening day of the hunting season are those that became pets during the previous summer. City hunters can't tell a tame deer from a wild one. They all look and behave alike to the unpracticed eye. I will not shoot a deer that has obviously been tamed, but unfortunately most hunters can't tell the difference. But don't criticize the hunter. The real killer is the misguided tourist who "tamed" the deer to stand in the presence of humans.

Another common error by the misinformed is the "rescue" of "abandoned fawns," a prime headache of game wardens. A spotted fawn is probably the most appealing of all animals. It is helpless, easy to approach. But it is *never* abandoned by its mother! It may be alone for a while, but never cast off. If you see such a fawn, take your pictures, admire it, then leave, or at least retreat some distance and watch. Chances are you'll see the doe return to pick up her offspring.

The problems wild things have with us humans is that we apply our standards to their lives. They are completely unreconcilable! The kindest act you can extend to a wild animal is *not* to stuff a marshmallow into its mouth. Admire it, photograph it, enjoy its presence. Then, if your concern for wildlife is genuine, put the fear of man into it! Hoot, holler, scream, whistle! Drive it away. Only in their natural state can wild animals survive.

Smaller animals can be pests, of that there's no doubt. Raccoons will tip over campground garbage cans, skunks will stroll through tentsites in search of bits of discarded waste foods, and campgrounds in wilderness areas may be visited regularly by bear, whose table manners are notoriously gauche. Chipmunks and squirrels will nibble at whatever food they find on picnic tables. Weasels, mink, and jays are thieves, although the smaller species are more likely to elicit laughter than fear or anger. The camper who learns to live with woodland critters enjoys a fascinating kaleidoscope of life. After all, the *camper* is the intruder.

Organized campgrounds, particularly as the summer wears on, are powerful attractions for wild animals. The tempting smells of foodstuffs are wafted long distances to critters who are not averse to an easy meal. Bits of food dropped on the ground and easily overlooked by humans are prized by tiny prowlers. Any camper who's ever paused by a bakery to relish the smell of freshly baked bread can appreciate the attraction a campground has for wild things.

SNAKES

I won't pretend that I *like* snakes. I'm not afraid of them, nor am I comfortable with them. On occasions (nature schools) I've had to handle live specimens, and because there were children, I tried to hide my apprehension. So I can understand the horror some folks feel at the sight of a snake. As a young guide I once had to overtake and physically restrain a woman from running hysterically into the woods when an eighteen-inch garter snake slithered into the clearing where we were enjoying our noon lunch.

I'm certain that a fear of snakes is transmitted from parent to child. Children are naturally unafraid of snakes. At nature training sessions I've seen youngsters reach eagerly forward for a five-foot indigo snake. My own daughter enjoyed holding and trying to control a six-foot boa constrictor! But mothers of these youngsters gasped in horror.

I'm not urging that snakes be considered potential pets—as most young boys would consider them—but that there is little to fear from them so far as campers are concerned. In areas where poisonous snakes are known to exist, commonsense precautions will help you avoid them. Don't put your hands into rocky crevices until you've investigated them, and when stepping over a log or rock, be sure the far side isn't already occupied. As for a poisonous, or otherwise, snake crawling into a tent, I've never heard of such an occurrence during more than thirty-five years under canvas. You won't have to stretch a horsehide rope around your shelter to keep out reptiles. They'll give you a wide berth, not only willingly, but anxiously.

The incidences of snake bites are rare, and then usually among professional handlers in zoos or research centers. Eleanor and I once enjoyed the sublime experience of prowling for several days in Okefenokee Swamp. Our minds had been conditioned by phony TV shows and movies to expect poisonous vipers to drop from branches into our boat or canoe (we used both). We approached alligators, dozens of them. We saw turkey vultures. Bear were around us. But snakes? We saw not a single one! They were there, some twenty-nine different species, but *they avoided us!*

INSECTS

Early summer is the season, at least in the North, with which I'm most familiar, for black flies, mosquitoes, midges, and "no-see-ums," the latter so tiny you'll feel their burning sting before you see them. Mosquitoes persist well into late summer, but the first cool night in late July usually tones down the harassment by the others.

Anyone who comes up with a formula for foiling these stinging pests will be awarded a niche in the Outdoorsmen's Hall of Fame. I can offer only the standard advice, the usual precautions: a tent equipped with netting; a recreational vehicle with tight screens; long-sleeved shirts; pants with cuffs tucked into stockings or boots; and copious use of repellents.

I generally rely on pipe smoke, but this doesn't help the ladies or the male nonsmoker. Just about all repellents are helpful, but none is completely effective. Cutter's is one of the most effective, either cream style or in aerosol cans. It is nongreasy, pleasantly scented, and popular among women. Eleanor swears by aerosol-type Off, especially the new Deep Woods version, also available as a cream. She keeps a half-dozen cans at Camp Hell 'n' Gawn and a couple more at our rural home.

I've used these, along with Old Woodsman, Lollacapop, 6-12, and a variety of home concoctions whose bases are generally citronella. They all help, but complete protection simply does not exist.

A partial solution to the problem is a smudge pot. Build a fire in a metal pail, then heap smoke-creating fuels into it—grass, leaves, punky wood, mosses. Locate the pail so that wind will carry the thin smokescreen through your campsite. Your eyes may smart, but it'll keep the bugs at bay!

Chapter 19

BEHAVIOR IN CAMP

I had originally planned to entitle this chapter "Crime in Camp." But frankly, I hate to admit that behavior problems are *that* serious in our camping areas. Unfortunately, they are. I might as well own up to it.

In 1966 I wrote in an earlier book: "There is rarely any need for a police officer on a campground . . . even petty crimes are notably absent."

Times have changed.

Since that date I've lost several items to thieves while camping: a sheath knife, playing cards, food, woods tools, and a lantern. My daughter and her husband had life-saver cushions stolen from their canoe when they left it for less than five minutes along a wilderness canoe route. I shrugged these minor losses off as "kid stuff." Then my utility trailer disappeared from its parking place along our woods road.

A friend, observing the owner of an expensive motor home emptying his holding tank into a trout stream, was told to "Mind your own business!" when he protested.

While Eleanor and I were camped at Furlong Bay Campground in British Columbia, one or more punks crashed their jalopy through the wooden gate (closed for the night to "protect" campers) and roared around the campground for several minutes before hurtling out onto the highway. (I longed for my shotgun and a load of No. 7½ shot!)

A criminologist, researching crime and vandalism on Wisconsin campgrounds, was robbed *three* times during a single summer. Among his losses were tape recordings of his findings!

In a national forest near my home, trail signs adjacent to highways are heavily greased on their back surfaces to discourage their removal as souvenirs.

In that same national forest, rangers recently had to call on state and local police, plus the sheriff's department, to control a mob of young pot smokers who had taken over and terrorized what had been a peaceful camping area.

At a Massachusetts nature school, I drove off a pair of prowlers who had been lurking around a Girl Scout encampment. I had my shotgun that night! And it was loaded.

These are trivial matters by FBI standards. They never appear in the annual crime report. But they can be terribly frightening to family groups.

Murder, armed robbery, and assaults, which rate space in the FBI recapitulations, are rare on campgrounds, so much so that when an isolated instance does occur, it rates sensational coverage in the news media.

Crime, however, is on the increase in campgrounds. The National Park Service does not maintain a special force of park police simply to protect the cookies on your picnic table. Nor does the Forest Service train employees to deal with theft, destruction of property, drug and alcohol abuse, and even assaults on officers, merely to expend its budget. There *are* problems.

I'm not suggesting that you give up camping. I don't intend to. When you consider the number of family campers abroad on any given weekend, or during the vacation season, the crime rate is extremely low. A campground lane is still safer than most city streets.

And we can enhance the peace of mind most of us seek in the outdoors. Two basic rules are essential.

1. Become involved. I don't mean that you should rush into a situation and make a citizen's arrest! Don't! Not unless you're a trained police officer. But if you observe suspicious behavior, or witness a violation, report it. Immediately. Even if you're not sure of yourself, remember that the police would rather respond to a false alarm than discover a crime when the culprit is miles away. Observe details: the make, year and color of the car, license number, general appearance and apparel of the culprits, the time and location of the crime—anything that may seem trivial may be important. And don't sneer at a backcountry deputy sheriff. He's probably as efficient in his environment as the finest TV detective is in his.

2. Take precautions. A common, and foolhardy practice is to camp overnight in highway rest stops. I don't mean the service areas along the interstate system but rather those roadside pulloffs along secondary and often isolated roads. Most states prohibit this sort of "camping." Delinquents of all types and inclinations cruise such roads at night, especially in rural areas, where

police patrols are spread far too thinly. Always camp only in authorized areas.

Once arrived at a campsite for a few days, you'll want to leave your rig or tent now and then for a swim at the beach or a hike in the woods. Leave nothing out in the open that might tempt thieves. A lantern, campstove, fishing tackle—any of these can disappear quickly. If you leave your car at the site, lock it, but don't leave valuables in sight. An expensive camera is safer in the glove compartment than on the front seat, even with the car locked. Leaving a radio playing softly in a recreational vehicle or in a tent will lead a casual thief to believe the place is occupied, and he'll continue on his way. Arrange with your camping neighbors to keep an eye on each other's outfits, a sort of campground community crime watch.

Should you have to leave your trailer unattended, especially in an isolated area where you are the only campers, the Master Lock Company has a device that locks over the coupler, making it virtually impossible for anyone to tow your outfit away. Had I used one of these I'd probably still have my utility trailer!

We've come to a sad day, indeed, when it is no longer prudent to leave camping equipment or other outdoor gear unprotected!

Readers of my newspaper camping column

Garbage and trash left in fireplace by a camper who didn't appreciate the beauty he defiled. RIVIERE

This lock slips easily over a trailer tongue socket to prevent theft of the unit. MASTER LOCK

occasionally ask me to suggest the best type of protection gun. Obviously, anyone who asks that question is not qualified to use one! My answer is always the same. The best gun is the one in a policeman's holster!

I know several family campers who carry a handgun, or more often, a shotgun, when they travel. If you are an expert, possibly an ex-policeman or a serviceman trained in the use of small arms, and the presence of a gun lends some feeling of security to your camping trip, by all means carry one.

Guns, however, usually create more problems than they prevent. A handgun permit in one state, for example, is not valid in another. An accidental discharge is always a possibility among those not familiar with firearms. Then there is the awesome decision: When is the use of a gun justified? Misjudge this and you may be charged with manslaughter! Also, do you want to risk a shoot-out with your wife and children present?

Unless you are an expert—and I don't mean a casual user who can hit a target three out of ten shots—forget about guns as a means of pro-

tection. I repeat: The best protective weapon is the one in a policeman's holster.

Incidentally, I am not opposed to the use of guns by sportsmen, target shooters, or even for home protection, but I am strongly opposed to the use of guns by persons who are not qualified. Experts rarely get into trouble. Amateurs do, continually.

I don't intend to make family camping these days seem like the Wild West of Jesse James' era. Incidents of violence are extremely rare. It's just that when they *do* occur, they get a big play in the news media *because they are unusual.* Campground problems on the whole are relatively minor, though sometimes more than annoying.

Wholesome family types are frequently guilty of callous and selfish behavior, often without realizing it. I once had to reprimand a father and son for ruining the tallest red spruce in our area by using it as a target for a hatchet-throwing contest. The father's apology could not have been more sincere. "There are so many trees," he explained, "I guess we didn't realize . . ." Campers who occasionally dug up small "Christmas trees" for transplanting to their lawns at home usually had the same explanation, And, chances are, the camper who takes a short cut across another's campsite will detour carefully at home to avoid treading on his neighbor's lawn. A double standard seems to evolve in the out of doors. What isn't permitted at home often becomes acceptable in the woods.

The bane of most campground managers and rangers is parents who fail to supervise their children. Mothers, for example, often send tots to the toilet house alone, and not once but several times during the four years that we operated a campground, we have had to clean human waste from toilet seats, compartment doors, and even walls. When we supplied bathroom tissue in rolls, we found great lengths of it draped over doors, clothes hooks, shower heads, and lavatories. So we switched to sheet dispensers. The paper was no longer draped. It was strewn like confetti. Youngsters play hide-and-seek in the shower stalls, and they leave the hot-water taps running. One year we added a rather expensive (we wanted a sturdy one that would last) croquet set to the play area for campers' use. Within three days, four of the six mallets had been broken. Every parent in the area was appalled at the thoughtlessness "of other kids."

Annoyance sometimes results from well-intentioned acts. Campers, thinking to relieve the rubbish collection tasks, frequently burn garbage in their fireplaces, and the horrible stench is then wafted about the campground. Since such wastes seldom burn completely, the chore boy then has to clean the fireplace following the "helpful" camper's departure. Another vexing problem is created by the camper who isn't satisfied with the location of his fireplace and builds a fire elsewhere. Worse yet, if the fireplace is of loose stone, he moves it—usually to the gravel pad, where another camper may want to pitch his tent.

Countless other trivial annoyances contribute to the needless shortening of tempers: a family squabble that can be heard for half an acre around; an off-color story that drifts clearly from a close-by campfire through the walls of your tent when children are retiring; nails driven into trees, difficult to pull out and waiting to scratch someone; the picking of wild flowers—not the plentiful daisies but the rare lady's slipper; the washing of supper dishes in the showerhouse lavatory; speeding on campground roads; loud coffee klatches that run well past midnight; even worse, the invariably louder and more boisterous beer party; the goofball who chops wood at 5 A.M.

This sort of thoughtlessness on a campground is not criminal in the legal sense. But it is common, a crime against good manners that depreciates an outdoor experience for all.

Pets are a problem, dogs especially. For years I went along with the theory that an indifferent minority maligned the many who control their pets. But I've now come to the conclusion that dogs have no place on a busy, highly compacted camping area. State and federal campgrounds, as well as most private facilities, require a leash. Some state parks ban dogs altogether.

Where leash regulations exist, most campers comply, but too many ignore them in the belief that "my dog is well behaved . . . he won't hurt anyone." I've seen a woman clawed by an overly friendly boxer and another whose hands were severely lacerated when she tried to pet a roaming, "friendly" terrier. Callously indifferent owners, too, won't bother to clean up droppings. I've noticed all too often that pet owners, when they "walk their dogs," do so away from their own campsite, then slink back when Rover has completed his chores! By day, campers comply with the campground rule requiring a leash, but at night they release their dogs to roam freely. The evidence is eloquent the next morning: garbage cans overturned and rubbish strewn about; food stolen from campers' tables or ruined; children frightened. Dogs barking at night are a special annoyance.

The sentiment against pets on campgrounds is becoming more widespread and outspoken, so it's wise to check beforehand whether or not you'll be welcome at a campground if your favorite boxer or Pomeranian is panting eagerly in the back seat.

If I were operating a family-type campground today, I'd ban dogs. There, I've said it!

Chapter 20

INSURANCE

Insuring camping equipment is closely related to car and home insurance because most campers tote their gear in an automobile or drive or tow a recreational vehicle. Certain provisions of home owners' or renters' policies may protect you on campgrounds.

However, neither a regular automobile policy, nor a home owners'-renters' policy is generally adequate without specific additional provisions. Frankly, it gets complicated.

There are two prime aspects of insurance for campers: (1) liability, property damage, and/or bodily injury; (2) physical damage or loss, comprehensive, and collision.

Under (1), liability, property damage, and/or bodily injury, your insurance company will pay claims against you, up to the limits of the policy, that may result when you are adjudged responsible for property damage, injury, or death.

"Up to the limits of the policy" are crucial words. If your policy is inadequate, and the judgment against you is greater than your policy coverage, the court will require that *you* pay the difference. If you accidentally back your truck camper into a neighbor's travel trailer, punching a hole in a side panel, a minimum-liability policy will cover the $500 repair bill. But suppose, while backing into a tight spot in a campground, you back your camping trailer into a curious tot and you injure him seriously so that he needs hospitalization. You may claim that the child had no business there. Your insurance company may agree, but if the child's parents bring suit against you, their attorney may bring in expert medical testimony that the child has been permanently injured. The court then makes a decision. If the case goes against you, and the court awards the parents $79,000, and your liability policy has a limit of only $50,000, *you* will pay the extra $29,000. This is a hypothetical case, an example, using relatively low figures. Today's courts are inclined toward much larger settlements when they involve serious injury, maiming, or extremely long hospitalization. Six-figure settlements are not unusual. Of course, your insurance company will fight the case for you, but, if you lose, it can pay only up to the policy limits. The balance is your responsibility. In the instance of a substantial settlement, your life savings could be wiped out, your home sold, and part of your salary taken from you for the rest of your life!

Many states require a minimum amount of liability insurance on automobiles, motor homes, and truck campers. Other states operate on a "financial responsibility" basis, which means that you are not required to buy liability insurance, but should you have a claim against you, you must prove that you are financially able to pay it. A few states are now under a "no fault" system, which is aimed at reducing the number of relatively small claims awaiting overcrowded courts. This system applies mostly to highway collisions, in which case each driver's insurance pays his damages without regard to determining which driver caused the accident. But this system does not eliminate court action in the case of bodily injuries or death.

The cost of liability insurance varies from area to area, the type of vehicle you drive, and the purposes for which you drive. However, the cost decreases as you increase coverage. In other words, the greater your coverage, the less per thousand it costs you. That first $100,000 may seem expensive, but the next $200,000 to $300,000 are bargains! It's like buying the large economy size.

Under (2), physical damage or loss, comprehensive, and collision provisions protect *you* from direct loss of your rig or equipment. The "physical damage or loss" applies to *your* outfit.

Some rather liberal policies are available, covering virtually every possibility of damage to your rig, or theft, including its contents. Group policies available to camping clubs and associations run as low as $2.25 per $100 of coverage. Individual, nonclub members will pay somewhat more. But even then, the cost is relatively low, considering the protection you obtain. For example:[1]

A windstorm flips your trailer over; someone breaks into your trailer and ransacks it; your cookstove "flares up" and sets fire to the rig; a flash flood ruins your clothing and equipment, and shoves your trailer against a tree; you burn out a wheel bearing on the highway and have to be towed in; a tree falls on your camper during a windstorm; you return to your campsite to find your trailer stolen; a highway accident smashes your rig and you have to spend a couple of nights in a motel while adjustments are being made; your spare tire is stolen; your hitch breaks and your trailer ends up in a ditch; you drive into a low-hanging branch and puncture your truck cab-over. . . .

Such policies also cover the contents of your unit, up to 10 per cent of its cash value. They also cover you in case of "falling aircraft," which is pretty far out, but flood, wind, theft, vandalism, and highway accidents, are real and very possible. Such insurance is a bargain.

Friends of ours, for example, had their new tent trailer rammed from the rear by a truck on

an expressway, the accident occurring as they headed gaily north for their annual vacation. They were uninjured, their car undamaged, but the trailer was a total loss. Highway police took them to a nearby service plaza, from which they called an agent of their insurance company. He was on the scene within an hour, arranging for a motel and meals, at the insurance company's expense. Before 9 A.M. the next day, an exact duplicate of their trailer was delivered to them.

One note of caution. No matter what type of wheeled rig you drive or haul, don't overlook the value of dealing with an insurance firm that specializes in recreational vehicle coverage. When a claim arises, the appraisal will be conducted by an adjuster who is familiar with this type of vehicle, its construction, and repairs. An automobile insurance claim usually involves work by a body shop and a mechanic. Your motor home, however, may need work by a body man, a mechanic, a plumber, and an electrician! It's a more complex vehicle.

As a rule, claims are paid "in kind or in cash," which means that the vehicle will be repaired, replaced at its current cash value, or you can accept a cash settlement.

Tenters, once the family car is suitably covered, have little need for additional liability coverage. After all, your tent isn't likely to fall on a passerby and injure him. But you can suffer losses from wind, flood, theft, or vandalism. Check your home owners' or renters' policy. You may be covered against such possibilities in that some policies consider a campsite as an extension of your home. But this is not *necessarily* so. Have your insurance agent appraise your needs, then ask him to point out the specific coverages your policy includes. If it lacks some, have them added.

Most of us begrudge every penny paid as insurance premiums, and certainly a discussion of the "insofars, hereinafters, and aforementioneds" isn't likely to contribute any degree of hilarity to a campfire gathering, but when the awful moment strikes and your camping gear is a mass of tangled wreckage, a pocketful of fine print is a comforting thing.

[1] This information is cited by the Foremost Insurance Company.

Chapter 21

CAMPING CLUBS

Frankly, I'm not a joiner. I dropped out of Rotary years ago because I became bored with chicken à la king and singing "Grandfather's Clock" every Tuesday noon.

As for camping clubs, my first meeting was a midwinter, Sunday afternoon, knee-deep-in-potato-salad affair. Some thirty youngsters spared neither sound nor gesture as cowboys and Indians killed each other off, spattering chocolate eclairs as they fell into dying spasms. I've no objection to western warfare in its place, but this particular fracas was centered among the members of the adult audience, who were trapped into listening to a latter-day Cecil B. DeMille narrate a nauseous film describing his "trip out West"—complete with out-of-focus views of Old Faithful, his cousin Mildred in Elmira, Mount Rushmore underexposed, his uncle Fenimore in Sioux City, the Little Big Horn battlefield blurred, his sister-in-law Hyacinth watering her petunias in Salt Lake City, and his wife Millicent waving coyly from her perch astride a stuffed grizzly bear in a roadside tourist trap.

This was followed by a synthetic soprano soloist, Strangula Stringent, who sang "I Could Have Danced All Night." The fire department, a block away, mistook her screeching for an alarm and responded with a hook-and-ladder truck, three pumpers, and a rescue unit. At this point I mustered a look of great urgency and slipped out an open window onto a fire escape, forgetting to renew my membership the next year. However, the experience didn't permanently embitter me against camping clubs. If such meetings were typical, I'd move for congressional action banning any assembly of campers. Fortunately, most camping groups accomplish considerably more than the organized consumption of casserole dishes.

In fact, their accomplishments are impressive. They've led antilittering programs that have cleaned up thousands of miles of roadsides; they have eliminated "permanent" camping in some state parks where seasonal renters had taken over campsites to the extent of planting vegetable gardens and installing electric refrigerators; they have even gone to the U. S. Supreme Court (still pending) to defend a recreational vehicle owner's right to park his rig in his driveway; they have organized "clinics" aimed at stopping the spread of the gypsy moth; they have pressured private campgrounds, and, in some cases, state areas, into raising facility standards; they have even come up with practical sanitary codes for state and private camping areas! They have pressured legislators, coddled and wheedled, at the state and national level, to the extent that many local chapters and/or members now serve as advisers to state park, forest, and recreation commissions.

The greatest failure of organized campers is their public-relations effort. The media rarely report their accomplishments. As a result, their image is distorted. Nonmembers sneer. I've heard camping groups referred to as "kooks in green jackets," a completely unfair and unwarranted allegation! The truth is that nonjoiners have benefited immeasurably from the efforts of their more gregarious brethren!

The group camp-outs, so often criticized by campers with more solitary inclinations, sometimes involve no fewer than twenty families, or they may take on the gargantuan proportions of the NCHA annual "Campvention," which attracts from seven thousand to ten thousand campers. Critics of such gatherings protest, "This isn't camping!" First to agree are the members who attend. These meetings are not intended to be occasions for solitude or close-to-nature experiences. They are, in reality, outdoor conventions—strictly fun. Once over, members go their separate ways to enjoy solitary camping or crowded campgrounds, as their tastes may dictate.

It's difficult for wilderness campers to understand the tendency of family campers to congregate in groups. The fact is that most campers have neither the experience nor the inclination for a back-of-beyond wilderness trip. True, a few are all-'round experts, but the majority are not only content with full campgrounds—they wouldn't have it otherwise. Most of them enjoy having other campers close by, and it's on the family campground that the coffee klatch has reached its zenith. To some degree the gregarious camper has the advantage over the lone wolf. Shunning fellow campers is becoming more difficult every day, since 90 per cent of our campgrounds are accessible by car. The fun and fellowship of organized family camping isn't altogether aimless, since some good must come from bringing together kindred spirits. Fortunately, whether or not you're a "joiner," there's plenty of room on both sides of the fence.

Certain other benefits accrue to members of clubs and associations. Nearly all publish some sort of bulletin that keeps the membership up to date on camping matters, both nationally and regionally. Some even publish full-fledged magazines that rival those of professional publishers. Members usually end up on mailing lists to receive catalogs issued by equipment dealers and outfitters. Discounts are sometimes offered.

The National Campers and Hikers Association[1] is the largest of the organized groups with chapters and individual members in every state. NCHA is quite intensely organized, all the way from the national to the local level. Anyone who wants to become active is likely to get an assign-ment on one of the many projects the association is usually carrying on. Whatever seems to need being done, NCHA membership becomes involved.

The next-largest group is the North American Family Campers Association,[2] formerly the New England Family Campers Association. NEFCA became NAFCA a few years ago when a growing number of campers from outside its area showed interest. So it "went national," and now has chapters in most states, and individual members in all. The association publishes its own camping magazine, *Campfire Chatter*, formerly available only to membership but now about to go on the newsstands.

Another lively group is the Family Motor Coach Association,[3] an organization of motor home and converted-bus owners. I've attended only one of their "conventions," in Vermont in 1972. I found an unusual camaraderie here, not only interest in each other as persons but an avid curiosity about the mechanics of converting and operating motor coaches. I saw rigs that ranged from regular Winnebagos, to Greyhound buses converted to personal and luxurious highway homes, to decrepit school buses being rebuilt to serve as family travel rigs. The association has state and regional chapters, which hold monthly rallies year-'round.

An unusual association is Loners on Wheels (LOW). Membership is open to any single camper/traveler, whether divorced, widowed, or just plain unmarried. Lest you conclude that there are "swinging" undertones, rest your suspicions. No member man and woman may travel together and camp in the same rig. The penalty is expulsion. If romance blossoms and there are wedding bells, the principals become *ex*-LOW members and may not fly its banner! LOW is strictly a fun group for those who might otherwise face loneliness. You can't fault that motivation!

The manufacturers of recreational vehicles have organized "clubs"[4] open to those who own and drive their rigs. While such groups appear to have a tinge of commercialism about them, they gather together thousands who have similar interests. The red numbers you see on the front of Airstreams have a significance. These num-

[1] See the Appendix.

[2] See the Appendix.
[3] See the Appendix.
[4] See the Appendix.

bers identify the driver to other Airstream owners as they pass each other. Each carries a directory in which names and hometowns are listed numerically. I cite Airstream, but there are several other such organizations nurturing mutual interest in highway rigs. In this day of cold indifference to each other on our roads, it's a nice thought that you can identify the camper who just passed you! Some of these "brand name" clubs also conduct organized tours—Wally Byam tours for Airstream and "Big W" for Winnebago are only two examples. There are others.

Regional, state, and local camping clubs, many of the latter sponsored by municipal recreation agencies, exist all over the country. They may or may not be associated with a national group.

Whether or not you choose to join, chances are you're enjoying better campsites and riding in safer camping rigs as a result of the efforts of organized campers.

While not a "consumer" organization, the Family Camping Federation,[5] a part of the American Camping Association, was originally proposed as an aid to professionals in the field. Back in the early sixties, when the FCF struggled to remain alive, it did, indeed, provide a genuine service. Then, as the camping boom developed, big business "came to the aid" of the

FCF. As a result, it is now little more than a public-relations showcase for Ford, General Motors, Coleman, KOA, and others who send executives to speak at seventy-five-dollar-a-day annual conventions at posh resorts and expensive city hotels.

Although not directly related to family camping, several organizations have much to offer family campers by way of environmental understanding. The fact that you camp in a fifteen-thousand-dollar motor home does not, I'm sure, indicate that you are indifferent about the preservation and restoration of our outdoor heritage. While you may never climb a mountain, run a severe rapids, or hike through a threatened wilderness, you may still want to help. Consider membership in such organizations as The Wilderness Society, the Sierra Club,[6] the Friends of the Earth, or a state or local conservation group. You may occasionally hear a spokesman for one of these speak out against the proliferation of recreational vehicles on certain public lands, but if you read and listen closely, you'll discover that their aims, and yours, are closely parallel.

Don't join every group that mails you an appeal. Pick out one that has special significance for you. Sign up. Support it. Backpackers and motor home campers have more in common than they realize!

[5] See the Appendix.

[6] See the Appendix.

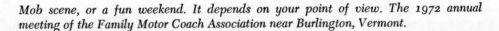

Mob scene, or a fun weekend. It depends on your point of view. The 1972 annual meeting of the Family Motor Coach Association near Burlington, Vermont.

Chapter 22

DO IT YOURSELF

The satisfaction that comes from making your own camping equipment or building your own recreational vehicle is twofold: You save money, and your gear is literally custom-made to your specifications. As a bonus, there's personal pride in the accomplishment.

Do-it-yourself projects are not for everyone. Some of us, unfortunately, are bumble fingers to whom changing a light bulb is a major chore. However, any woman who gets along reasonably well with a sewing machine can come up with superb outdoor clothing, ditty bags, sleeping bags, even tents. Today's lightweight and easy-to-work nylons facilitate the work.

Any man handy with tools, and using the many prefabricated parts and sections that are available, can build a professional-looking camper.

For lightweight camping gear, such as day packs, frames, sleeping bags, and small tents, excellent directions are given in the book *Lightweight Camping Equipment and How to Make It.*[1]

Even if you're not directly interested in this type of equipment, this volume contains excel-

[1] Gerry Cunningham and Margaret Hansson (Denver, Colo.: Gerry Division, Outdoor Sports Industries, Inc., 1974).

Precut fabric and components for a down-filled do-it-yourself jacket.
FROSTLINE

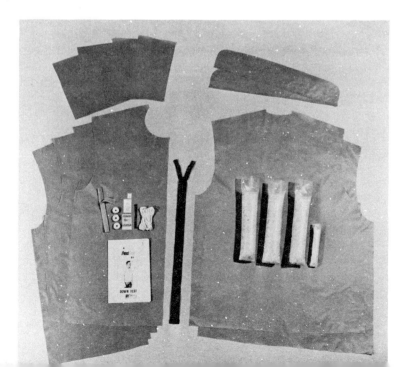

Practical yet stylish outdoor jackets available in kit form. FROSTLINE

terials, threads, buttons, zippers, and other necessities, notably those of Frostline, Inc., and the Holubar Company.[2] These are also aimed primarily at the backpacker, but much of this type of clothing is nicely adaptable to family camping.

Kits are offered by the Viking Camper Supply Company[3] for converting vans into mini motor homes and buses into personal highway coaches. The firm also has kits for building slide-in and chassis-mount truck campers, chopped vans, travel trailers, and even a fifth-wheel trailer. The use of such kits eliminates that "homemade" look and, of course, interior designs can be adapted to suit your tastes exactly.

For the more skillful do-it-yourselfer who would rather build a unit from scratch, plans can be obtained from the Trail-R-Club of America[4] for camping trailers, truck caps, travel trailers, slide-in and chassis-mount truck campers, and for the conversion of Volkswagen, Ford, Dodge, or Chevrolet vans. Components for recreational vehicles make a "from scratch" project easily feasible, these sold by such firms as C. P. Products Corporation.[5] Virtually any item necessary to produce a complete camper of any type is available, including hardware, interior and exterior lights, heaters, bath and kitchen accessories and appliances, plus all sorts of piping, fittings, and wiring.

[2] See the Appendix.
[3] See the Appendix.
[4] See the Appendix.
[5] See the Appendix.

lent instructions for laying out patterns, cutting, and sewing, including the various stitches that are suitable for clothing headed for rough outdoor work.

Too, there are kits for making outdoor clothing, and sleeping bags, consisting of precut ma-

A homemade rig? Yes, from a kit. VIKING

APPENDIX

BUREAU OF INDIAN AFFAIRS, Dept. of the Interior, 1951 Constitution Ave., N.W., Washington, D.C. 20242. Also:

820 Main St., Aberdeen, S.D. 57401

5301 Central Ave., N.E., Albuquerque, N.M. 87108

Federal Bldg., P.O. Box 368, Anadarko, Okla. 73005

316 N. Twenty-sixth St., Billings, Mont. 59101

Box 3-8000, Juneau, Alaska 99801

831 Second Ave., S., Minneapolis, Minn. 55402

Federal Bldg., Muskogee, Okla. 74401

Navajo Area Office, Window Rock, Ariz. 86515

124 W. Thomas Rd., Phoenix, Ariz. 85011

1425 N.E. Irving St., Portland, Ore. 97208

2800 Cottage Way, Sacramento, Calif. 95825

BUREAU OF LAND MANAGEMENT, Dept. of the Interior, Washington, D.C. 20240. Also field offices:

7981 Eastern Ave., Silver Spring, Md. 20910

555 Cordova St., Anchorage, Alaska 99501

Federal Bldg., Phoenix, Ariz. 85025

Federal Bldg., Sacramento, Calif. 95814

Federal Bldg., Denver, Colo. 80202

Federal Bldg., Boise, Idaho 83702

Federal Bldg., Billings, Mont. 59101

Federal Bldg., Reno, Nev. 89502

Federal Bldg., Santa Fe, N.M. 87501

729 N.E. Oregon St., Portland, Ore. 97208

Federal Bldg., Salt Lake City, Utah 84111

Federal Bldg., Cheyenne, Wyo. 82001

BUREAU OF RECLAMATION, Dept. of the Interior, Washington, D.C. 20240. Also regional offices:

Region 1: 550 W. Fort St., Box 8008, Boise, Idaho 83707

Region 2: Federal Bldg., Sacramento, Calif. 95825

Region 3: Nevada Highway and Park St., Box 427, Boulder City, Nev. 89005

Region 4: 125 S. State, Box 11568, Salt Lake City, Utah 84111

Region 5: Herring Plaza, 317 E. Third, Box 1609, Amarillo, Tex. 79105

Region 6: 316 N. Twenty-sixth St., Box 2553, Billings, Mont. 59101

Region 7: Bldg. 20, Denver Federal Center, Denver, Colo. 80225

CORPS OF ENGINEERS, Dept. of the Army, Chief of Engineers, Washington, D.C. 20314. Also district offices:

Dist. 1: P.O. Box 1538, Albuquerque, N.M. 87103

Dist. 2: P.O. Box 1715, Baltimore, Md. 21203

Dist. 3: Foot of Bridge St., Buffalo, N.Y. 14207

Dist. 4: P.O. Box 905, Charleston, S.C. 29402

Dist. 5: 219 S. Dearborn St., Chicago, Ill. 60604

Dist. 6: P.O. Box 1027, Detroit, Mich. 48231

Dist. 7: P.O. Box 1600, Ft. Worth, Tex. 76101

Dist. 8: P.O. Box 2127, Huntington, W. Va. 25701

Dist. 9: P.O. Box 4970, Jacksonville, Fla. 32201

Dist. 10: 1800 Federal Bldg., Kansas City, Mo. 64106

Dist. 11: P.O. Box 867, Little Rock, Ark. 72203

Dist. 12: P.O. Box 17277, Foy Station, Los Angeles, Calif. 90017

Dist. 13: P.O. Box 59, Louisville, Ky. 40201

Dist. 14: 668 Federal Office Bldg., Memphis, Tenn. 38103

Dist. 15: P.O. Box 1169, Mobile, Ala. 36601

Dist. 16: P.O. Box 1070, Nashville, Tenn. 37202

Dist. 17: 424 Trapelo Rd., Waltham, Mass. 02154

Dist. 18: P.O. Box 60267, New Orleans, La. 70160

Dist. 19: 111 East Sixteenth St., New York, N.Y. 10003

Dist. 20: 6012 U. S. Post Office and Court House, Omaha, Neb. 68101

Dist. 21: Custom House, Second and Chestnut Sts., Philadelphia, Pa. 19106

Dist. 22: 564 Forbes Ave., Manor Bldg., Pittsburgh, Pa. 15219

Dist. 23: 628 Pittock Block, Portland, Ore. 97205

Dist. 24: Clock Tower Bldg., Rock Island, Ill. 61202

Dist. 25: P.O. Box 1739, Sacramento, Calif. 95808

Dist. 26: 180 New Montgomery St., San Francisco, Calif. 94105

Dist. 27: P.O. Box 889, Savannah, Ga. 31402

Dist. 28: 1519 S. Alaskan Way South, Seattle, Wash. 98134

Dist. 29: 906 Oliver St., St. Louis, Mo. 63102

Dist. 30: 1217 U. S. Post Office and Custom House, 180 E. Kellog Blvd., St. Paul, Minn. 55101

Dist 31: P.O. Box 61, Tulsa, Okla. 39181

Dist. 32: P.O. Box 60, Vicksburg, Miss. 39181

Dist. 33: Bldg. 602, City-County Airport, Walla Walla, Wash. 99632

Dist. 34: P.O. Box 1890, Wilmington, N.C. 28402

FOREST SERVICE, U. S. Dept. of Agriculture, Washington, D.C. 20250. Also regional offices:

Region 1: Federal Bldg., Missoula, Mont. 59801

Region 2: Federal Center, Bldg. 85, Denver, Colo. 80225

Region 3: 517 Gold Ave., S.W., Albuquerque, N.M. 87101

Region 4: 324 Twenty-fifth St., Ogden, Utah 84401

Region 5: 630 Sansome St., San Francisco, Calif. 94111

Region 6: 319 S.W. Pine St. (P.O. Box 3623), Portland, Ore. 97208

Region 8: 1720 Peachtree Rd., N.W., Atlanta, Ga. 30309

Region 9: 633 W. Wisconsin Ave., Milwaukee, Wis. 53203

Region 10: Federal Office Bldg. (P.O. Box 1628), Juneau, Alaska 99801

NOTE: Region 7 was not accidentally omitted. It was eliminated some years ago when combined with another region.

NATIONAL PARK SERVICE, Dept. of the Interior Building, Washington, D.C. 20240. Also regional offices:

North Atlantic Region: Maine, New Hampshire, Vermont, Massachusetts, Rhode Island, Connecticut, New York, and New Jersey: 150 Causeway St., Boston, Mass. 02114

Mid-Atlantic Region: Pennsylvania, Maryland, West Virginia, Delaware, and Virginia: 143 South Third St., Philadelphia, Pa. 19106

National Capital Parks: Metropolitan area of Washington, D.C.: 110 Ohio Drive S.W., Washington, D.C. 20242

Southeast Region: Alabama, Florida, Georgia, Kentucky, Mississippi, North Carolina, South Carolina, Tennessee, Puerto Rico, and the Virgin Islands: 3401 Whipple St., Atlanta, Ga. 30344

Midwest Region: Ohio, Indiana, Michigan, Wisconsin, Illinois, Minnesota, Iowa, Missouri, Nebraska, and Kansas: 1709 Jackson St., Omaha, Neb. 68102

Rocky Mountain Region: Montana, North Dakota, South Dakota, Wyoming, Utah, and Colorado: 645–655 Parfet Ave., Denver, Colo. 80215

Southwest Region: Arkansas, Louisiana, New Mexico, Oklahoma, and Texas: Old Santa Fe Trail, Santa Fe, New Mex. 87501

Western Region: Arizona, California, Nevada, and Hawaii: 450 Golden Gate Ave., San Francisco, Calif. 94102

Pacific Northwest Region: Alaska, Idaho, Oregon, and Washington: 1424 Fourth Ave., Seattle, Wash. 98101

BUREAU OF SPORT FISHERIES and WILDLIFE, Dept. of the Interior, Washington, D.C. 20240. Also regional offices:

Box 3737, Portland, Ore. 97208

Box 1306, Albuquerque, N.M. 87103

1006 West Lake St., Minneapolis, Minn. 55408

809 Peachtree-Seventh Bldg., Atlanta, Ga. 30323

U. S. Post Office and Court House, Boston, Mass. 02109

SUPERINTENDENT OF DOCUMENTS, U. S. Government Printing Office, Washington, D.C. 20402

TENNESSEE VALLEY AUTHORITY (TVA), Public Information Office, Knoxville, Tenn. 37902; or Woodward Building, Fifteenth and H Sts., Washington, D.C. 20444. Also Division of Reservoir Properties:

530 New Sprankle Bldg., Knoxville, Tenn. 37902

135 W. First St., Morristown, Tenn. 37814

516 W. Madison St., Athens, Tenn. 37303

601 First Federal Bldg., Muscle Shoals, Ala. 35660

202 W. Blythe St., Paris, Tenn. 38242

STATE AGENCIES

ALABAMA: Bureau of Publicity and Information, State Highway Dept. Bldg., Montgomery, Ala. 36104

ALASKA: Dept. of Economic Development, Alaska Travel Div., Pouch E, Juneau, Alaska 99801

ARIZONA: Travel Information Section, Dept. of Economic Planning and Development, Suite 1704, 3003 N. Central Ave., Phoenix, Ariz. 85012

ARKANSAS: State Parks, Recreation and Travel Commission, 149 State Capitol, Little Rock, Ark. 72201

CALIFORNIA: Office of Tourism and Visitor Services, 1400 Tenth St., Sacramento, Calif. 95814

COLORADO: Colorado Travel Development, 602 State Capitol Annex, Denver, Colo. 80203

CONNECTICUT: State Park and Forest Commission, 165 Capitol Ave., Hartford, Conn. 06115

DELAWARE: Dept. of Natural Resources and Environmental Control, Div. of Parks, Recreation, and Forestry, P.O. Box F, Dover, Del. 19901

DISTRICT OF COLUMBIA: National Capital Region, National Park Service, 1100 Ohio Drive, S.W., Washington, D.C. 20242

FLORIDA: Dept. of Natural Resources, Education, and Information, J. Edwin Larson Bldg., Tallahassee, Fla. 32304

GEORGIA: Dept. of State Parks, 270 Washington St., S.W., Atlanta, Ga. 30334

HAWAII: Hawaii Visitors Bureau, 2285 Kalakaua Ave., Honolulu, Hawaii 96815; Dept. of Land and Natural Resources, Div. of State Parks, P.O. Box 621, Honolulu, Hawaii 96809

IDAHO: Dept. of Commerce and Development, Rm. 108, State Capitol Bldg., Boise, Idaho 83707

ILLINOIS: Tourism Div., Dept. of Business and Economic Development, 222 S. College St., Springfield, Ill. 62706

INDIANA: Dept. of Natural Resources, Div. of State Parks, 616 State Office Bldg., Indianapolis, Ind. 46204; Indiana Tourist Div., 336 Statehouse, Indianapolis, Ind. 46204

IOWA: Public Relations, State Conservation Commission, 300 Fourth St., Des Moines, Ia. 50319

KANSAS: Dept. of Economic Development, State Office Bldg., Topeka, Kan. 66612; State Park and Resources Authority, 801 Harrison, Topeka, Kan. 66612

KENTUCKY: Dept. of Public Information, Travel Div., Capitol Annex Bldg., Frankfort, Ky. 40601

LOUISIANA: State Parks and Recreation Commission, P.O. Drawer 1111, Baton Rouge, La. 70821

MAINE: Maine Publicity Bureau, Gateway Circle, Portland, Me. 04102; State Park and Recreation Commission, State House, Augusta, Me. 04330; Maine Forest Service, Augusta, Me. 04330

MARYLAND: Dept. of Forests and Parks, State Office Bldg., Annapolis, Md. 21404

MASSACHUSETTS: Dept. of Natural Resources, Div. of Forests and Parks, Box 1775, Boston, Mass. 02105

MICHIGAN: Michigan Tourist Council, Suite 102, 300 S. Capitol Ave., Lansing, Mich. 48926

MINNESOTA: Div. of Parks and Recreation, Centennial Office Bldg., St. Paul, Minn. 55101; Minnesota Vacations, 51 E. Eighth St., St. Paul, Minn. 55101

MISSISSIPPI: Mississippi Park System, 717 Robert E. Lee Bldg., Jackson, Miss. 39201

MISSOURI: Missouri State Park Board, Box 176, Jefferson City, Mo. 65101; Missouri Tourism Commission, P.O. Box 1055, Jefferson City, Mo. 65101

MONTANA: Advertising Dept., Montana Highway Commission, Helena, Mont. 59601

NEBRASKA: Nebraskaland, State Capitol, Lincoln, Nebr. 68509

NEVADA: Nevada State Park System, Rm. 221, Nye Bldg., 201 S. Fall St., Carson City, Nev. 89701

NEW HAMPSHIRE: Div. of Economic Development, P.O. Box 856, Concord, N.H. 03301

NEW JERSEY: State Promotion Section, P.O. Box 400, Trenton, N.J. 08625; Dept. of Environmental Protection, Div. of Parks, Forestry, and Recreation, P.O. Box 1889, Trenton, N.J. 08625

NEW MEXICO: State Park and Recreation Commission, Box 1147, Santa Fe, New Mex. 87501; Tourist Division, Dept. of Development, 113 Washington Ave., Santa Fe, New Mex. 87501

NEW YORK: New York State Dept. of Environmental Conservation, Div. of Lands and Forests, Albany, N.Y. 12201; Park Information, Parks, and Recreation, Bldg. 2, State Campus, Albany, N.Y. 12226

NORTH CAROLINA: Travel and Promotion Div., Dept. of Conservation and Development, Raleigh, N.C. 27611

NORTH DAKOTA: Travel Div., North Dakota State Highway Bldg., Capitol Grounds, Bismarck, N.D. 58501

OHIO: Dept. of Natural Resources, Div. of Parks and Recreation, 913 Ohio Departments Bldg., Columbus, O. 43215; Ohio Development Dept., Information Central, Box 1001, Columbus, O. 43216

OKLAHOMA: Oklahoma Tourism Division, 500 Will Rogers Bldg., Oklahoma City, Okla. 73105

OREGON: Travel Information Section, State Highway Dept., Salem, Ore. 97310

PENNSYLVANIA: Bureau of State Parks, Rm. 601, Feller Bldg., 301 Market St., Harrisburg, Pa. 17101; Travel Development Bureau, 402 South Office Bldg., Harrisburg, Pa. 17120

RHODE ISLAND: Rhode Island Development Council, Tourist Promotion Div., Roger Williams Bldg., 49 Hayes St., Providence, R.I. 02908

SOUTH CAROLINA: Dept. of Parks, Recreation, and Tourism, Box 1358, Columbia, S.C. 29202

SOUTH DAKOTA: Travel Div., Dept. of Highways, Pierre, S.D. 57501

TENNESSEE: Div. of State Parks, Dept. of Conservation, 2611 West End Ave., Nashville, Tenn. 37203

TEXAS: Parks and Wildlife Dept., John H. Ragan Bldg., Austin, Tex. 78701; Texas Highway Dept., P.O. Box 5064, Austin, Tex. 78703

UTAH: Utah Travel Council, Council Hall, Capitol Hill, Salt Lake City, Utah 84114

VERMONT: Dept. of Forests and Parks, Montpelier, Vt. 05602

VIRGINIA: Div. of Parks, State Office Bldg., Richmond, Va. 23219; Virginia State Travel Service, 911 E. Broad St., Richmond, Va. 23219

VIRGIN ISLANDS: Virgin Islands National Park, Box 806, Charlotte Amalie, V.I. 00801

WASHINGTON: Visitor Information Bureau, General Administration Bldg., Olympia, Wash. 98501

WEST VIRGINIA: Div. of Parks and Recreation, Dept. of Natural Resources, State Office Bldg., Charleston, W.VA. 25305

WISCONSIN: Vacation and Travel Service, Dept. of Natural Resources, Box 450, Madison, Wis. 53701

WYOMING: Wyoming Travel Commission, 2320 Capitol Ave., Cheyenne, Wyo. 82001

CANADIAN AGENCIES

CANADIAN GOVERNMENT TRAVEL BUREAU, 150 Kent St., Ottawa 4, Ont., Canada. Also:

263 Plaza, Prudential Center, Boston, Mass. 02199

100 North LaSalle St., Chicago, Ill. 60602

Room 1010, Enquirer Bldg., 617 Vine St., Cincinnati, O. 45202

Winous-Point Bldg., 1250 Euclid Ave., Cleveland, O. 44115

Book Bldg., 1257–1259 Washington Blvd., Detroit, Mich. 48226

510 West 6th St., Los Angeles, Calif. 90014

124 South 7th St., Northstar Center, Minneapolis, Minn. 55402

680 Fifth Ave., New York, N.Y. 10019

Suite 305, Three Penn Center, Philadelphia, Pa. 19102

1001–3 Jenkins Arcade, Liberty and Fifth Avenues, Pittsburgh, Pa. 15222

247 Midtown Plaza, Rochester, N.Y. 14604

600 Market St., Suite 2300, San Francisco, Calif. 94104

Suite 1117, Plaza 600, 600 Stewart St., Seattle, Wash. 98101

RCA Bldg., 1725 K St., N.W., Washington, D.C. 20006

ALBERTA: Travel Alberta, 10255 104 St., Edmonton, Alta. T5J 1B1

BRITISH COLUMBIA: Dept. of Travel Industry, 1019 Wharf St., Victoria, B.C. V8W 2Z2

MANITOBA: Dept. of Tourism, Recreation and Cultural Affairs, Tourist Branch, 491 Portage Ave., Winnipeg, Man. R3B 2E7

NEW BRUNSWICK: Dept. of Tourism. P.O. Box 1030, Fredericton, N.B. E3B 5C3

NEWFOUNDLAND and LABRADOR: Tourist Services Division, Dept. of Tourism, Confederation Bldg., St. John's, Nfld. A1C 5T7

NORTHWEST TERRITORIES: Div. of Tourism, Dept. of Economic Development, Yellowknife, N.W.T. X0E 1H0

NOVA SCOTIA: Nova Scotia Dept. of Tourism, P.O. Box 130, Halifax, N.S. B3J 2M7

ONTARIO: Ministry of Industry and Tourism, Parliament Bldgs., Toronto, Ont. M7A 1T3

PRINCE EDWARD ISLAND: Tourist Information Centre, Dept. of Environment and Tourism, P.O. Box 940, Charlottetown, P.E.I. C1A 7M5

QUEBEC: Dept. of Tourism, Fish and Game, Place de la Capitale, 150 E. Blvd. Saint-Cyrille, Quebec, P.Q. G1R 2B4

SASKATCHEWAN: Tourist Branch, Dept. of Tourism and Renewable Resources, 7th Floor, SPC Bldg., Regina, Sask. S4P 2Y9

YUKON TERRITORY: Dept. of Tourism and Information, P.O. Box 2703, Whitehorse, Y.T. Y1A 2C6

MEXICO

MEXICAN GOVERNMENT TOURIST DEPARTMENT, 625 N. Michigan Ave., 12th Floor, Chicago, Ill. 60611

PRIVATE CAMPGROUND OWNERS' ASSOCIATIONS[1]

ARKANSAS
Sherlon and Laurine Hilliard
Camp Lake Hamilton
Route 1 Box 559
Hot Springs 71901

CALIFORNIA
California Campground Owners' Association
Marvin D. Wadley
2672 Cottage Way
Sacramento 95825

COLORADO
Colorado Campground Association, Inc.
P.O. Box 965
Colorado Springs 80901

CONNECTICUT
Connecticut Campground Owners' Association
Ann Daly, Secretary
Killingly 06239

DELAWARE
Delaware Recreational Park Owners' Association
212 South Shore Drive
Dover 19901

FLORIDA
Florida Association of Camping and Trailering Parks
Cecil S. Farrar, Executive Secretary
P.O. Box 5841
Sarasota 33579

GEORGIA
Georgia Campground Owners' Association
Mrs. Ralph Gilbert, Secretary
Route 1, Box 36
Midland 31820

IDAHO
Idaho Campground Association
Tony Zornik, President
Route 5, Box 370
Idaho Falls 83401

ILLINOIS
Association of Illinois Rural Recreation Enterprises
Pat Huck, Secretary
Route 1, Box 178
Troy 62294

[1] Courtesy of Campground and RV Park Management, P.O. Box 1014, Grass Valley, Calif. 95945

INDIANA
Hoosier Outdoor Recreation Association
Wayne Dillman, President
c/o R.R. 5
Greencastle 46135

IOWA
Iowa Association of Private Campground Owners
Harold Mills, President
Breezy Ridge Campground
Afton 50830

MAINE
Maine Co-operative Camping Areas
Everett Leland, Executive Director
South Lebanon 04027

MARYLAND
Maryland Association of Campgrounds
Clyde A. Morris, President
Freeland 21053

MASSACHUSETTS
Massachusetts Association of Campground Owners
Barbara Wilgus, Secretary
200 Hillside Road
Westfield 01085

MICHIGAN
Michigan Association of Private Campground Owners
E. Lee Goucher, President
P.O. Box 125
Jones 49061

MINNESOTA
Minnesota Association of Campground Owners, Inc.
Richard V. Ward, President
Box 334
Elk River 55330

MISSISSIPPI
Mississippi Campground Owners' Association
Bill Howie, President
1100 Cowan Road
Handsboro Station
Gulfport 39501

MISSOURI
Missouri State Campground Owners' Association
John B. Campbell, President
1518 N.W. Vivion Road
Kansas City 64118

MONTANA
Campground Owners' Association of Montana
Ken Bailey, President
Box 188
Somers 59932

NEBRASKA
Nebraska Association of Private Campground Owners
Lee Whitehead, President
Kamperville
Route 2
Cozad 69130

NEW HAMPSHIRE
New Hampshire Campground Owners' Association
Roy B. Heise, Executive Director
R.D. 3
Winchester 03470

NEW JERSEY
New Jersey Private Campgrounds Association
Edwin Risdon, President
R.D. 1, Box 104-H
Tuckerton 08087

Cape May County Campgrounds Association
Box 608
Ocean View 08230

NEW YORK
Campground Owners of New York
R.D. 2, Box 421
Endicott 13760

NORTH CAROLINA
North Carolina Campground Owners' Association
R. C. "Tim" Malone
Green Acres RFD
Williamstown 27892

Outer Banks Campground Owners' Association
Bill Booker
Sandpiper's Trace, Box 442
Manteo 27954

OHIO
Ohio Campground Owners' and Operators' Association
P.O. Box 376
Worthington 43085

PENNSYLVANIA
Campground Association of Pennsylvania
Denis Snyder, President
Bald Eagle Campground
R.D. 3, Box 230
Tyrone 16686

RHODE ISLAND
Rhode Island Campground Owners' Association
Alton Bassett, President
Ginny B Campground
Foster 02825

SOUTH CAROLINA
South Carolina Private Campground Owners' Association
J. Rut Connor, President
Rocks Pond Campground
Eutawville 29048

Myrtle Beach Family Campground Association
Don Herring, President
Lake Arrowhead, Star Route
Myrtle Beach 29577

SOUTH DAKOTA
South Dakota Campground Owners' Association
Don Richards, President
1035 Lawrence Street
Belle Fourche 57717

TEXAS
B. L. McDonald
McDonald Farms Campground
Route 1
Arp 75770

UTAH
Utah Private Parks Association
Bob Olds, President
Willard Bay Kampground
516 North Second East Street
Brigham City 84302

VERMONT
Vermont Association of Private Campground Owners and Operators
Morris LaFrance, President
Lake Champagne
Randolph Center 05061

VIRGINIA
Virginia Campground Association
W. O. Giles, Secretary
Route 1
Union Hall 24176

WEST VIRGINIA
West Virginia Campground Owners' Association
Mrs. Roselle Leatherman, Secretary
Falling Waters Campsite
Falling Waters 25419

WISCONSIN
Wisconsin Association of Campground Owners
Box 191
Wisconsin Dells 53965

WYOMING
Wyoming Campground Owners' Association
William Parish
Hyland Trailer Park
Cheyenne 82001

CAMPING EQUIPMENT MAKERS AND SUPPLIERS

NOTE: The following lists of recreational vehicle makers, camping equipment manufacturers, and suppliers is not complete. Only those to whom I have referred in the book are included. A listing does not imply recommendation of the product, nor does an omission indicate disapproval. There simply isn't room for a complete list!

BEAN, L. L., Freeport, Me. 04032

CAMP-A-TOASTER, 74 Vine St., East Providence, R.I. 02914

COLEMAN COMPANY, THE, Wichita, Kans. 67201

DULUTH TENT AND AWNING COMPANY, 1610 West Superior St., Duluth, Minn. 55806

DUPONT COMPANY, 350 Fifth Ave., New York, N.Y. 10001

EUREKA TENT AND AWNING COMPANY, P.O. BOX 966, Binghamton, N.Y. 13902

FROSTLINE, INC., P.O. Box 2190, Boulder, Colo. 80302

GLOY'S, INC., 11 Addison St., Larchmont, N.Y. 10538

GRISWOLD MANUFACTURING COMPANY, P.O. Box 261, Sidney, O. 45365

HOLUBAR, Box 7, Boulder, Colo. 80302

HUDSON'S BAY COMPANY, Hudson's Bay House, 77 Main St., Winnipeg 2, Man. R3C 2R1, Canada

LAACKE AND JOYS COMPANY, 1432 North Water St., Milwaukee, Wis. 53202

NATIONAL CANVAS PRODUCTS, Camping and Sporting Goods Div., P.O. Box 2268, Central Station, Toledo, O. 43603

OPTIMUS, AB, INC., 652 East Commonwealth, Fullerton, Calif. 92634

PAULIN PRODUCTS COMPANY, 30520 Lakeland Blvd., Willowick, O. 44094

PRIMUS-SIEVERT, 354 Sackett Point Rd., P.O. Box 502, North Haven, Conn. 06473

RAEMCO, INC., Box 482, Somerville, N.J. 08876

SEARS, ROEBUCK AND COMPANY, 303 East Ohio, Chicago, Ill. 60611

SHEEPHERDER STOVE: The Smilie Company, 575 Howard St., San Francisco, Calif. 94105

SIMS STOVES, Lovell, Wyo. 82431

THERMOS DIVISION, King-Seeley/Thermos Company, Norwich, Conn. 06360

TRAILBLAZER/WINCHESTER, Taylorville Rd., Statesville, N.C. 28677

TRAILCOOKER CAMP KITCHEN: IHA, INC., 51 Lake St., Nashua, N.H. 03060

WENZEL, A., TENT AND DUCK CO., St. Louis, Mo. 63132

ZEBCO DIVISION, Brunswick Corporation, P.O. Box 270, Tulsa, Okla. 74101

RECREATIONAL VEHICLE MAKERS AND ALLIED SUPPLIERS

AIRSTREAM, Church St., Jackson Center, O., 45334; also 15939 Piuma Ave., Cerritos, Calif. 90701

APACHE: The Vesely Company, P.O. Box 370, Lapeer, Mich. 48446

ARGOSY MANUFACTURING COMPANY, 60 Vista Rd., Versailles, O. 45380

CHAMPION HOME BUILDERS, 5573 E. North St., Dryden, Mich. 48428

CHEVROLET RV Buyer's Guide, P.O. Box 7271, Detroit, Mich. 48202

CHRYSLER-PLYMOUTH, P.O. Box 7749, Detroit, Mich. 48207

COACHMAN INDUSTRIES, INC., P.O. Box 30, Middlebury, Ind. 46540

CORSAIR TRAVEL VEHICLES, 2746 LaMontte St., Marlette, Mich. 48453

C. P. PRODUCTS CORPORATION, 1611 West Bristol, Elkhart, Ind. 46514

COX CAMPERS, Grifton, N.C. 28530

DEL REY INDUSTRIES, INC., 3910 Cassopolis, Elkhart, Ind. 46514

DODGE: Trucks and Recreational Vehicles, P.O. Box 857, Detroit, Mich. 48231

EAZ-LIFT, P.O. Box 489, Sun Valley, Calif. 91352

FAN COACH CO., LaGrange, Ind. 46761

FORD MARKETING CORP., Box 1000, Dearborn, Mich. 48121

FRANKLIN COACH CO., INC., Nappanee, Ind. 46550

GRUMMAN MOTOR HOMES, 600 Old Country Rd., Garden City, N.Y. 11530

HARVEST RECREATIONAL VEHICLES, INC., 1204 No. Santa Anita Ave., South El Monte, Calif. 91733

HI-LO TRAILER CO., 100 Elm St., Butler, O. 44822

HYLAND MANUFACTURING CO., P.O. Box R, Carlisle, I. 50047

KARDEL, BMC, FREEZER INSERT AND CAMPER CLAMPER: Blackstone Manufacturing Company, 4630 West Harrison St., Chicago, Ill. 60644

LIFETIME MOTOR HOMES, P.O. Box 1708, Mason City, I. 50401

MASTER LOCK CO., Milwaukee, Wis. 53245

NIMROD, 500 Ford Blvd., Hamilton, O. 45011

PALOMINO: Vanguard Industries, Savage, Minn., 55378; also Colon, Mich. 49040

PUMA CAMPERS: Ski-Tow Manufacturing Company, 3301 Phillips St., Elkhart, Ind. 46514

SAFE-T-TOW, P.O. Box 201, Halesite, N.Y. 11743

SHASTA INDUSTRIES, Simi, Calif. 93065

SKAMPER CORPORATION, Bristol, Ind. 46507

SPORTSMOBILE, 1063 Main St., Andrews, Ind. 46702

STARCRAFT CORP., Goshen, Ind. 46526

STEURY CORPORATION, 310 Steury Ave., Goshen, Ind. 46526

SUPERIOR MOTOR HOMES, Div. of Sheller-Globe Corp., Lima, O. 45802

TRAIL KING, New Rd., Lenni, Pa. 19014

TRAIL-R-CLUB OF AMERICA, Box 1376, Beverly Hills, Calif. 90213

TRAVEL MATE: Travel Equipment Corporation, P.O. Box 512, Goshen, Ind. 46526

TURTLE TOPS INC., 118 West Lafayette St., Goshen, Ind. 46526

VALLEY TOW RITE, P.O. Box 850, Lodi, Calif. 95240

VIKING CAMPER SUPPLY COMPANY, INC., 99 Glenwood Ave., Minneapolis, Minn. 55403

CAMPING AND RECREATIONAL VEHICLE PERIODICALS

Camper Coachman, 10148 Riverside Drive, North Hollywood, Calif. 91602

Campfire Chatter, Box 248, Littleton, Mass. 01460

Camping Guide, 319 Miller Ave., Mill Valley, Calif. 94941

Camping Journal, 229 Park Ave. S., New York, N.Y. 10003

Family Motor Coaching, P.O. Box 44144, Cincinnati, O. 45244

Trailer Life, 10148 Riverside Drive, North Hollywood, Calif. 91602

Trailer Topics, 28 East Jackson Blvd., Chicago, Ill. 60604

Trailer Travel, 500 Hyacinth Place, Highland Park, Ill. 60035

Wheels Afield, 8490 Sunset Blvd., Los Angeles, Calif. 90069

MAJOR MEMBERSHIP AND SERVICE ORGANIZATIONS

FAMILY MOTOR COACH ASSOCIATION, P.O. Box 44144, Cincinnati, O. 45244

FAMILY CAMPING FEDERATION, Bradford Woods, Martinsville, Ind. 46151

LONERS ON WHEELS, Mrs. Edith Lane, 2940 Lane Drive, Concord, Calif. 94518

NATIONAL CAMPERS AND HIKERS ASSOCIATION, 7172 Transit Rd., Buffalo, N.Y. 14221

NORTH AMERICAN FAMILY CAMPERS ASSOCIATION, P.O. Box 552, Newburyport, Mass. 01950

RECREATIONAL VEHICLE INSTITUTE, O'Hare Office Center, 2720 Des Plaines Ave., Des Plaines, Ill. 60018

CAMPING-TRAVEL ASSISTANCE AGENCIES

CAMPING GUIDE TOURS, INC. (worldwide), Rt. 1, Box 877, Grass Valley, Calif. 95945

CARAVANAS de MEXICO (Mexico), 3801 B North Piedras, El Paso, Tex. 79930

CONTINENTAL CAMPERS, INC., 84 State St., Boston, Mass. 02109 (Western Europe); also: Amsterdam Woods Campsite, Post Box 7580, Schiphol Oost, Amsterdam, Netherlands

OLD WAGONMASTER CARAVANS (Mexico), 10920 Brookfield Rd., Chatsworth, Calif. 91311

POINT SOUTH CARAVAN TOURS, 5309 Garden Grove Ave., Tarzana, Calif. 91356

SANBORN'S (Mexico), 2001 South Tenth St., McAllen, Texas 78501

WILSON'S MOTOR CARAVAN CENTER (Western Europe), Acre Lane, London S.W. 2, England

WOODALL TRAIL CLUB (Mexico and Europe), 2870 Skokie Valley Rd., Highland Park, Ill. 60035

NOTE: Most major airlines and travel agents will assist you in planning a camping trip almost anywhere in the world!

SANITARY STATION DIRECTORIES

RAJO PUBLICATIONS, 319 Miller Ave., Mill Valley, Calif. 94941 (small charge)

WOODALL PUBLISHING COMPANY, 500 Hyacinth Place, Highland Park, Ill. 60035 (*Trailering Park & Campground Directory*, available in most bookstores)

FRANCHISE CAMPGROUNDS

NOTE: Franchised campgrounds "come and go"! Except for a few successful ventures in this field, the franchising of campgrounds has a history of instability. The following are those that appear to be "here to stay" and that were in operation at the time of this writing.

CRAZY HORSE CAMPGROUNDS, 2152 DuPont Drive, Newport Beach, Calif. 92664

HOLIDAY INN TRAV-L-PARKS, Trav-L-Park Dept., Holiday City, Memphis, Tenn. 38118

KAMPGROUNDS OF AMERICA, INC., Billings, Mont. 59103

OUTDOOR RESORTS OF AMERICA, INC., 311 Plus Park Blvd., Nashville, Tenn. 37217

RED ARROW, 88 Steele St., Denver, Colo. 80206

SAFARI CAMPS OF AMERICA, P.O. Box 454, Columbia, Mo. 65201

VENTURE OUT IN AMERICA, INC. (Gulf Oil Corp.), 3445 Peachtree Rd., N.E., Atlanta, Ga. 30326

BOTTLE GAS REFILL STATION DIRECTORIES

NATIONAL L-P GAS ASSOCIATION, 79 West Monroe St., Chicago, Ill. 60603 (small charge)

RAJO PUBLICATIONS, 319 Miller Ave., Mill Valley, Calif. 94941 (small charge)

HIGHWAY BUSES FOR CONVERSION

CONTINENTAL TRAILWAYS, 315 Continental Ave., Dallas, Tex. 75207

GREYHOUND LINES, 371 Market St., San Francisco, Calif. 94106; or: 1400 West Third St., Cleveland, O. 44113

RECREATIONAL VEHICLE INSURANCE

NOTE: Part of the insurance information outlined earlier in this book was made available by the following insurance firm. There are, however, several nationally represented companies supplying insurance of this type.

FOREMOST INSURANCE COMPANY, 5800 Foremost Drive, Grand Rapids, Mich. 49501

OTHER ORGANIZATIONS OF INTEREST TO FAMILY CAMPERS

AMERICAN FOREST INSTITUTE, 1319 Eighteenth St., N.W., Washington, D.C. 20036

AMERICAN RIVER TOURING ASSOCIATION, 1016 Jackson St. Oakland, Calif. 94607

AMERICAN YOUTH HOSTELS, 20 West Eleventh St., New York, N.Y. 10011

NATIONAL AUDUBON SOCIETY, 950 Third Ave., New York, N.Y. 10022

NATIONAL PARKS AND CONSERVATION ASSOCIATION, 1701 Eighteenth St., N.W., Washington, D.C. 20009

NATIONAL WILDLIFE FEDERATION, 1412 Sixteenth St., N.W., Washington, D.C. 20036

NATURE CONSERVANCY, THE, 1800 North Kent St., Arlington, Va. 22209

SIERRA CLUB, THE, 1050 Mills Tower, San Francisco, Calif. 94104; also:

250 West Fifty-seventh St., New York, N.Y. 10019

235 Massachusetts Ave., N.E., Washington, D.C. 20002

430 Auditorium Bldg., 427 West Fifth St., Los Angeles, Calif. 90013

2014 East Broadway, Rm. 16, Tucson, Ariz. 85719

4534½ University Way, N.E., Seattle, Wash. 98105

Box 5-425, College, Alaska 99701